PRAISE FOR GRIEVING THE WRITE WAY FOR SIBLINGS

"In times when we don't know how to express how we're feeling, writing the words can help - but so few of us know where to start. This book provides calming guidance and helpful information, along with prompts for writing or even saying aloud what we feel. There are few heartbreaks like losing a sibling. This book helps us navigate that."

—Kelli Levey Reynolds,
Communicator in Central Texas

"Finally, a book specifically for grieving siblings. Gary Roe has given us clear direction in the writing prompts to journey through this unique grieving experience. I will be highly recommending it in my grief ministry."

—Lyn Wagner,
GriefShare Facilitator

"Grieving the Write Way for Siblings is another superb book by Gary Roe. A must-read for those who have lost a sibling. Gary takes one through the various aspects of the grief journey when losing a sibling – emotionally, mentally, physically, spiritually, and relationally – allowing one to experience the benefits of writing about their loss in order to process grief in an effort to recover, adjust, heal, and grow."

—Joe N. Roop, bereaved spouse,
father, and sibling (twin to Jerry)

Grieving the Write Way for Siblings will be a helpful tool to get to the heart of the pain after the loss of a sibling. When my oldest sister died of cancer three years ago, this book would have helped me process the many emotions being left behind in a grieving family. The writing prompts in the book help you put a "handle" on the huge pot of questions and feelings. This book will be helpful to the often-forgotten members in grief after the loss of a child, the siblings. By your own hand, you will be your own companion and "safe" person to get "inside" and "get it out" and reach what is stuck in your emotional tank of grief. I recommend this book to anyone going through the loss of a sibling now or anyone that feels any residue of grief and sorrow after the loss of a sibling, no matter how long it has been. This would also be a great tool for a support group facilitator to use the questions to get to the heart of healing, for any type of loss.

—Wanda Stein,
Co-founder of Helping Hand Grief Support
and Living Through Suicide

"I am thrilled to have the opportunity to recommend *Grieving the Write Way for Siblings*. I am a retired minister who has counseled those who are grieving and have led Grief Groups for over 30 years. Gary Roe has written many books on grief that I have recommended and used with those I have counseled. When I began to read this workbook, I did so with the idea that I could find something that would be of help to a grieving person that has lost a sibling.

What I wasn't ready for was how this workbook was 'written for me.' The workbook stirred feelings of loss that will occur sometime in the future, whether it be for my twin sister or myself. I began to think how I might feel, and I wasn't ready for that. Thus, I recommend this workbook for all siblings, not just those currently grieving. I believe it would help us to not take our siblings for granted. Ask yourself, 'Is it time to begin to mend any brokenness between us, or even share with our siblings how much they mean to us while we still have each other?' Thank you, Gary, for helping me understand how much my sister means to me."

—Rev. Louie Lyon,
Retired United Methodist Minister

"This is an important book as there are very few books related to adult sibling grief that have been written by a 'grief expert'. Siblings are often considered forgotten grievers, especially adult siblings. Gary has done an amazing job of helping grieving adult siblings find ways to write out their memories and deal with their current emotions and struggles related to their sibling's death through a variety of journaling exercises. This book provides you an active role in engaging in your healing. Not only has he lost his only sibling, but Gary has engaged with many adults who have had siblings die, and this book is a product of all those interactions."

—Lisa Watson, Hospice Bereavement Coordinator
grieving the loss of her older brother

"As a police chaplain, I have been taken on scene where death has just happened. Once I conducted a funeral service for a gentleman where his one sibling was the only family member there and the only one who cried. Each death assaults a different part of the heart. Both my wife and I each have walked through the death of two siblings and both parents – even an infant grandson. Gary does a masterful job offering tools to walk us through this process. Our hearts need to be dealt with so that we can focus appropriately on the relationships of those still around."

— Tom Montgomery, MA,
Clergy and Police Alliance, Fort Worth Police

"Although it has been 57 years since my brother died, a remark by my daughter made me realize that my family and I had never really dealt with it. This is the book I wish I'd had as a 15-year-old. Losing my 17-year-old brother suddenly to a brain tumor shook my whole world and changed the dynamic of my family fundamentally. Writing my thoughts to the questions posed in this book would have been immensely helpful to my young self. There is no reason not to do so now, however. The gift of written reflection cannot be overestimated."

—Wendy Peters

"After losing my brother unexpectedly, this book is a great tool to help in moving forward and working toward healing. The writing prompts give readers an opportunity to have a free flow of information. Writing is cathartic anyway, and this book helps reflect and assist in processing the loss of a sibling and aids in truly thinking about the relationship you shared with them. I especially liked the section that provides ideas of ways to honor your loved one. While grieving is different for everyone, these exercises are insightful for those of us who have lost someone very special. Such writing exercises reinforce that it's up to us to move toward living a life with passion and purpose, something that we know our siblings would have wanted for us."

— Laura Shepherd-Madsen,
honoring her older brother, Dan

"It is so hard to lose your brother or sister and the accompanying emotions can be overwhelming, leaving you left behind and desperate for relief. *Grieving the Write Way for Siblings* is a workbook that offers thought provoking questions and ample space to jot down your responses to the sadness, doubts and questions that the death of a sibling brings. Having lost both, my sister and brother, I found this work very helpful in processing my grief for them."

—Floy Creveling

"I appreciated this new book as a resource for my sons who, as children, suffered the death of their baby sister and experienced the surrounding grief in our household. They are now adults and I hope this tool can help them process their grief at this stage in their lives. I hope they will find it useful to remember their sister and have a tool to process their grief as they age. Thank you, Gary, for helping us build our "grief toolkits" during the myriad ways that we encounter death, dying and losses."

—Aileen Carrell

GRIEVING
the ~~Right~~ **Write**
WAY
FOR SIBLINGS

A Practical Grief Workbook

GARY ROE

TABLE OF CONTENTS

Thank you for purchasing *Grieving the Write Way for Siblings*.

These pages are designed to be a companion for you as you grieve the loss of your sister or brother. Please don't go through this workbook just once. Pick it up again in six months or a year.

Come to it again and again. Each time you will be at a different place. You'll see your progress. You'll be encouraged. And you'll find your hope has grown.

As a thanks, please accept this gift – a free eBook (PDF):

Grief: 9 Things I Wish I Had Known

Download yours today:

https://www.garyroe.com/grief-9-thingsi-wish-i-had-known-ebook/

OTHER BOOKS BY GARY ROE

THE COMFORT SERIES

*Comfort for Grieving Hearts: Hope and
Encouragement in Times of Loss*

*Comfort for the Grieving Spouse's Heart: Hope
and Healing After Losing Your Partner*

*Comfort for the Grieving Adult Child's Heart:
Hope and Healing After Losing Your Parent*

*Comfort for the Grieving Parent's Heart: Hope
and Healing After Losing Your Child*

THE GOD AND GRIEF SERIES

Grief Walk: Experiencing God After the Loss of a Loved One

Widowed Walk: Experiencing God After the Loss of a Spouse

Broken Walk: Experiencing God After the Loss of a Child

*Orphaned Walk: Experiencing God After
the Loss of a Parent (coming soon)*

THE GOOD GRIEF SERIES

*The Grief Guidebook: Common Questions,
Compassionate Answers, Practical Suggestions*

Shattered: Surviving the Loss of a Child

*Hope in a World Gone Mad: Finding God
in Grief, Fear, and Anxiety*

Aftermath: Picking Up the Pieces After a Suicide

Teen Grief: Caring for the Grieving Teenage Heart

*Please Be Patient, I'm Grieving: How to Care
for and Support the Grieving Heart*

Heartbroken: Healing from the Loss of a Spouse

*Surviving the Holidays Without You: Navigating
Loss During Special Seasons*

THE DIFFERENCE MAKER SERIES

*Difference Maker: Overcoming Adversity and Turning
Pain into Purpose, Every Day (Adult & Teen Editions)*

*Living on the Edge: How to Fight and Win the Battle
for Your Mind and Heart (Adult & Teen Editions)*

WHAT THIS BOOK
IS ALL ABOUT

Your world has changed. Your family has been altered.

Your sibling is no longer here.

This loss hits you on all levels: emotional, mental, physical, spiritual, and relational.

Your routine has been upended. Life for you is not business as usual.

How could this happen?

What does this loss mean for you?

Who are you now?

What's next?

MY PERSONAL HISTORY WITH
WRITING AND GRIEF

I experienced multiple, traumatic losses in early childhood. By the time I was a teenager, I was slogging through each day carrying massive weights that I was unaware of.

Then I lost my dad. He dropped in front of me of a heart attack. He was a single dad and my one functional parent.

My grief burden was already massive. When this lightning bolt struck, I thought my life was over.

I was stunned.

I managed to stay functional. I went to school. I stayed on the swim team. I kept connecting with my friends. Because of previous losses, however, I already felt different from my peers. Now, I felt like I lived alone in some alternate universe.

One day I picked up a pencil and started writing. A poem materialized.

I wasn't a poetry fan, but somehow it fit my mood that day.

The next day, I wrote another poem. A few days later, I penned another.

Emotion began to spill out as I wrote. I cried. I paced and talked to myself. I yelled and screamed.

Writing poetry opened an avenue for my heart to express its anguish. Sadness, confusion, anger, fear, anxiety, and guilt spewed out of me, one word at a time. I felt lousy but expressing myself felt good and relieving.

I continued writing poetry throughout high school. In college, I began to journal. When I was upset or frustrated, I found myself writing down what I was feeling and thinking.

Keeping a journal became a habit. Writing about what was happening in my heart and mind became a part of my daily routine. I continue this today.

I write in the morning, before the pressures and interruptions of the day begin their assault. I get to process what happened yesterday. I prepare myself for today.

As a grief recovery author, grief specialist, and grief coach, I'm around death, loss, and heavy grief every day. I use writing to process and release the huge amount of pain that I hear and see.

Writing becomes especially valuable to me when I experience another loss - and there have been many losses throughout the decades. When my brother, my only sibling, died last year, writing again became key to my recovery and healing.

Frankly, I don't know what I would do without writing as a way of processing the pain, difficulties, and losses of life.

WRITING AND THE GRIEF PROCESS

Writing can play a massive part in the grief and healing process.

Writing steadies our hearts enough to express our emotions in a healthy and productive way.

Writing slows our spinning minds down enough to get our thoughts on paper and begin to process them.

Writing can enable us to consider the physical impact of grief on our bodies and help us decide what to do about it.

Writing gives us a safe place to express and process spiritual questions, doubts, and fears.

Writing allows us to share our frustrations about our relationships in an honest and uncensored manner.

Writing enables us to consider and work through our thoughts, wonderings, and fears about the future.

Writing can become a powerful habit that can help us navigate life in general. What we don't express stays locked in our hearts and often becomes some of the baggage that weighs us down.

Writing can be a tool which unveils hope. Hope is always here, but sometimes pain can blind us to it.

HOW THIS BOOK CAN HELP

This book is about you and the terrible loss you're enduring.

This book is about helping you express your heart, mind, and soul.

This book can aid you in tackling (in a sane and healthy way) all the changes that have been thrust upon you.

This book can assist you in navigating all the relational changes and upsets you're facing.

This book can help you honor your sibling as you grieve.

This book can help you see that you're not alone, you're not crazy, and that you will make it through this.

This book can help you take the next steps in your grief process, whatever they might be.

WELCOME TO *GRIEVING THE WRITE WAY FOR SIBLINGS*

So, welcome to *Grieving the Write Way for Siblings*. In the following pages, you'll get many opportunities to experience the benefits of writing about your loss and what's happening in your heart and mind.

As you move through the material, you'll find yourself getting more comfortable with journal writing using prompts.

You'll discover how to use letters and stories to process losses and other life events.

You'll dabble in the creative process of writing poetry. Even if you're not a poetry fan, I'm hoping you'll be surprised and pleased by what you get out of it.

I'm glad you're here. Take the next step. Read on…and write.

PART ONE:
THE EMOTIONAL OVERWHELM

The loss of a sibling hits our hearts.

Emotions rise from deep within us. These feelings
are powerful and can hijack our lives.

Emotional overwhelm is common.

How do you deal with this?

This section is designed to help you process the tremendous
emotional impact the death of a brother or sister can have. As
you read and write, breathe deeply from time to time. Express
your heart, as best you can. Be as real and as honest as possible.

1
"WHAT JUST HAPPENED?"

"I'm stunned. I'm in shock. What just happened?"

- B.W.

--------⊷⊖⊶--------

When a brother or sister dies, the shock waves can be immense.

Even if this death was expected, nothing can adequately prepare us for our sibling's final breath. That moment brings a whole new reality to our lives.

Perhaps our minds replay their passing over and over again.

Some of us have trouble accepting or even grasping the magnitude of what has just taken place.

In many cases, our sibling was a peer. A new realization of our own mortality comes crashing in upon us.

Every situation and each sibling loss is different. Perhaps you took care of them growing up, or they watched out for you. Maybe you were their caregiver at the end of their life.

Perhaps you were close to them. Maybe you felt distant from them. Perhaps your relationship was competitive, adversarial, or even estranged.

Maybe your sibling relationship looked good on the outside, but inside it was difficult. Perhaps you felt inferior or superior to them. Maybe you just didn't like them all that much.

Family relationships can be wonderful, challenging, and difficult - and everything in-between.

Whatever the case, this death is massively significant. Your sibling's passing will alter your family. It will change you too.

Take a moment to think about your relationship with your sibling. How would you describe it?

_____

_____

_____

_____

_____

_____

_____

_____

What was it that made your relationship the way it was? What were some of the contributing factors?

_____

_____

_____

_____

_____

_____

_____

_____

Writing Prompts:

Use the following to write more about your relationship with your sibling and how it is affecting you:

"When I think of my sibling's death, I feel..."

_____

_____

_____

_____

_____

_____

_____

_____

"My sibling's death has altered my family. Here are some of the things I've noticed..."

_____

_____

_____

_____

_____

_____

_____

_____

"When I think of my sibling today, what comes to mind is...."

_____

_____

_____

_____

_____

_____

_____

_____

_____

_____

_____

_____

_____

_____

_____

_____

The death of a sister or brother is stunning. You might go in and out of shock in the days ahead. Getting in touch with what's happening inside you and expressing your grief in healthy ways will be key to your recovery, healing, and personal growth.

2

"SAYING GOODBYE IS MORE IMPORTANT THAN I IMAGINED"

"I wasn't there. I didn't get to be with them. Saying goodbye is more important that I imagined."

- K.A.

When a sibling dies, that moment in time is etched into our minds and hearts. We will forever recall where we were and what we were doing.

Some get to be with their sibling at the time of death. Others do not.

Some get to say goodbye to their siblings because the death was expected. Others don't get this opportunity because their sibling died suddenly.

Some get to say everything they want and need to say. Others either don't get this chance or hold back for some reason.

In every case, how our sibling died, where, when, and how much we were able to be involved in that time naturally sticks with us. Yes, it was what it was, but it still had a huge impact on us.

Though every situation is unique, one thing is clear: saying goodbye is massively important.

Where were you when your sibling died? What were you doing?

_____

_____

_____

_____

_____

_____

_____

What else do you remember about that time?

_____

_____

_____

_____

_____

_____

_____

_____

_____

Writing Prompts:

Use the following to process more about the time of your sibling's passing. Try to write freely without editing. Try not to censor yourself in any way, but rather be as honest as possible:

"When my sibling died, I wish I had..."

_____

_____

_____

_____

_____

_____

_____

"When my sibling died, I'm glad I was able to..."

_____

_____

_____

_____

_____

_____

_____

If you were able to say goodbye to your sibling, what do you remember saying at that time? If you were not able to say goodbye, what would have said if you had the chance? Take some time on this. Be as thorough as you can.

_____

_____

_____

_____

_____

_____

_____

_____

_____

_____

_____

_____

Saying goodbye, either before your sibling's death or after, is crucial. We need as much closure as we can get. In fact, most of us will say goodbye many times in many ways. Saying goodbye is not so much an event as a process.

Our hearts need time to heal. This is as it should be. Be patient with yourself and this grief process.

3

"NO ONE KNEW HIM LIKE I DID"

"We grew up together. No one knew him like I did."

- M.H.

Each person - every sibling - is one-of-a-kind in human history, even if they're a twin.

Every sibling relationship is unique.

Therefore, no one knew your sibling like you did. There has never been another sibling relationship like yours, and there never will be again.

No wonder this hurts.

No wonder this is frustrating, confusing, and highly emotional.

No wonder this is hard - very, very hard.

You had a unique relationship with your brother or sister. No one else saw them exactly like you did. That makes your grief special, but also lonely.

Think about your sibling for a moment. Make a list of words below that describe them:

_____

_____

_____

_____

_____

Writing Prompts:

Use the writing prompts below to talk about your sibling. Try not to hold back. Let your heart speak.

"Some things I really appreciated and loved about my sibling were..."

_____

_____

_____

_____

_____

_____

_____

_____

"If I was going to describe my sibling to someone who didn't know them, I would make sure to tell them..."

_____

_____

_____

_____

_____

_____

_____

_____

Memory Writing Exercise:

Make a quick list of memories that are unique to you and your sibling (things you did together, conversations, events, etc.):

_____

_____

_____

_____

_____

_____

_____

_____

Choose one of the memories above and write more about that. "Tell the story" of that memory:

_____

_____

_____

_____

_____

_____

_____

_____

_____

_____

_____

_____

_____

_____

_____

_____

_____

_____

_____

_____

_____

_____

_____

_____

No one knew your sibling the way you did. Sharing memories about them is healthy and healing. You need to talk about them. Begin to look for ways and opportunities to share about your sibling with others - memories, what they said and did, etc. Their story needs to be told.

4

"THE EMOTIONS ARE OVERWHELMING"

"My feelings are all over the place. Ever since my sister
died, the emotions have been overwhelming."

– M.B.

───────◆─◇◆◇─◆───────

After the death of a sibling, powerful emotions can surge up within us.
Our feelings can be so intense that they begin to dominate our lives
and routines.

Feeling emotionally overwhelmed is common for those grieving
the loss of a sister or brother.

Sadness, confusion, frustration, anger, guilt, fear, anxiety, and depression come at us in waves. Some waves are smaller and easier to
navigate than others. Some temporarily knock us off our feet. Others
overwhelm us.

In grief, the waves just keep coming. If we get a break, it's not for
very long.

In our world, mood is king. How we feel in the present moment
tends to govern what we do and how. After the loss of a sibling, emotions tend to expand and take up more space. Intense feelings can
hijack us in an instant.

Feeling emotionally overwhelmed at times is a common experience for surviving siblings.

Take a moment and list some of the feelings and emotions that you have experienced since the death of your sibling:

_____

_____

_____

_____

_____

_____

_____

_____

Of these, which feelings have been the most challenging for you?

_____

_____

_____

_____

_____

_____

_____

_____

Writing Prompts:

Begin by completing the sentence and then free yourself to keep writing about whatever comes to mind.

"When I feel emotionally overwhelmed, I find myself wondering..."

_____

_____

_____

_____

_____

_____

_____

"When I'm hijacked by my feelings, I tend to respond by..."

_____

_____

_____

_____

_____

_____

_____

You may feel overwhelmed at times. That's okay. You're grieving the loss of your sibling. Be patient with yourself and handle what you can, one thing at a time.

5

"IT'S ALL SO SAD."

"I can't believe it. I talked to him just hours before his death.

It's all so sad. I'm so sad."

– D.E.

<hr>

Sadness is the most common of all the grief emotions.

Your sibling has died. Your family and your world have been altered. Sadness is a natural result.

This new sadness can be like a stabbing pain to the heart. It can also feel like a constant, dull ache.

Our sadness can resemble a heavy cloud that seems to cover everything.

Your sibling is no longer here. That's shocking and disorienting. Your heart has been hit. Sadness is spilling out.

Processing the sadness within you and "getting it out" is important. Your sadness honors your sibling. Expressing that sadness is one way of saying, "I love you."

How would you describe sadness? Try to write a simple definition:

_____

_____

_____

_____

_____

_____

_____

Think of some of the times you've felt sad since your sibling died. Describe one (or a couple) of these times:

_____

_____

_____

_____

_____

_____

_____

_____

_____

_____

_____

Writing Prompts:

Begin by completing the sentence and then keep writing about whatever comes to mind.

"When I think about my sibling's death, I feel sad about..."

_____

_____

_____

_____

_____

_____

_____

"When I feel sad about my sibling, I usually..."

_____

_____

_____

_____

_____

_____

Feeling sad is natural after the loss of a sister or brother. Take your heart seriously and express your sadness in healthy ways. Your sadness is your heart saying, "I love you."

6

"EVERYTHING SEEMS TO REMIND ME"

"Since my brother's death, everything seems to remind me of him. I even think I hear his voice or see him sometimes."

– P.L.

When a sibling dies, our hearts grieve. The pain of missing them can be enormous.

As time passes, we long to be with them (if we had a good relationship). We want what we had.

We long to see their face.

We long to hear their voice.

We long to be with them.

Everything seems to remind us of them. They are never far from our hearts and minds.

Expressing the longings within you is healthy and healing. Let your heart speak.

If our relationship with our sibling wasn't good, we mourn what we didn't have and perhaps wish that things had been different.

As you think about the loss of your sibling, what do you sense your heart is longing for (whether your relationship was good or not, our hearts long for many things)?

_____

_____

_____

_____

_____

_____

_____

_____

_____

_____

_____

_____

_____

_____

_____

_____

_____

Writing Prompts:

Begin by completing the sentence and then write about whatever comes to mind.

"When I think of you (my sibling), my heart longs to..."

_____

_____

_____

_____

_____

_____

_____

_____

_____

"Today, I wish I could..."

_____

_____

_____

_____

_____

_____

_____

_____

Memory Writing Exercise:

When you think about what you long for, what memories of your sibling come to mind? Pick one memory that seems to be strongest in your heart today. Write about that memory below. Don't evaluate or edit. Just write. Let your heart express itself.

_____

_____

_____

_____

_____

_____

_____

_____

_____

_____

_____

_____

_____

_____

_____

_____

_____

_____

_____

_____

_____

_____

_____

_____

_____

_____

_____

_____

_____

_____

_____

_____

_____

_____

_____

_____

When we lose someone, our hearts naturally long for the good we had. Expressing these longings is good, healthy, and healing. Let your heart speak.

7

"I'M AFRAID OF WHAT MIGHT HAPPEN NEXT"

"My sister's death has shaken me. I'm afraid of
what might happen next and to whom.

I don't like this."

– T.S.

————————

Immediately after the death of a sibling, we're in shock. We're stunned and perhaps even immobilized. As hours and days go by, a stark reality begins to dawn on us. If this can happen, what else might?

We wonder what's ahead. How are we going to do this? What's next?

A sense of powerlessness can emerge. On some level, we become aware that anything can happen to anyone at any time - even to us.

Fear begins to surface.

The death of a sister or brother can give birth to fears we've never had before.

Fear is powerful. At times, it might threaten to overwhelm us and take over our lives. Fear can drive our thoughts and decisions.

Fear is a part of the grieving process. As such, it needs to be acknowledged and expressed. When we're honest about what's happening inside us, we can then process and release our fears over time.

Look inside your heart. What fears are lurking there? What are you afraid of?

List your fears here:

_____

_____

_____

_____

_____

_____

_____

_____

_____

_____

_____

_____

_____

_____

_____

_____

_____

_____

Writing Prompts:

Begin by completing the sentence and then keep writing about whatever comes to mind.

"Since the death of my sibling, I find myself fearful that..."

_____

_____

_____

_____

_____

_____

"When I'm afraid, I typically respond by..."

_____

_____

_____

_____

_____

_____

_____

Fear is common in grief. Acknowledging and expressing fears as they arise is important and healthy.

8

"I'M DEFINITELY MORE ANXIOUS."

"I'm definitely more anxious. It's like I'm waiting for the next
disaster to strike. I feel like I'm on guard all the time now."
– F.Y.

———————————

When we experience the loss of a sibling, our anxiety level automatically rises.

Our lives have been shaken. Our personal worlds have been altered. Our family will never be the same.

We will never be the same.

This is shocking and unnerving. Anxiety is a natural result.

We can experience increased nervousness. Many have anxiety or panic attacks. We can feel worried, fearful, and shaky inside.

Managing grief anxiety is a challenge. The first key is remembering that we are not alone. High anxiety is natural and common for those on the grief journey.

Breathing deeply is a simple skill that can aid us greatly in handling the anxiety that comes. After the "Writing Prompts" section of this chapter, you will find a detailed explanation of helpful breathing skills that you can easily apply to daily life.

What do you tend to get anxious about? Make a list. Be as specific as you can.

_____

_____

_____

_____

_____

_____

_____

_____

When you feel anxious, what do you tend to do next? How do you handle that anxiety?

_____

_____

_____

_____

_____

_____

_____

_____

Writing Prompts:

Begin by completing the sentence and then express freely what comes to your heart and mind.

"Since my sibling died, I'm more anxious about..."

_____

_____

_____

_____

_____

_____

_____

"When anxiety strikes, I wish I could respond by..."

_____

_____

_____

_____

_____

_____

_____

Handling grief anxiety can be a bit like riding a roller coaster. Acknowledging and working through the anxiety is healthy for your heart, mind, and body.

GRIEF SKILL
THE HABIT OF DEEP BREATHING

The habit of deep breathing is an important grief skill. Those who practice it regularly have found it extremely helpful in managing the volatile thoughts and emotions that are part of the grief journey.

Breathe in deeply through your nose and then out through your mouth. As an EMT friend of mine says, "Smell the roses, blow out the candles." This activates your parasympathetic nervous system and brings a calming effect to your brain and body.

Breathe deeply and slowly for a couple of minutes. Focus as much as possible on your breathing. Close your eyes if necessary.

Consider practicing deep breathing twice a day - once at the beginning of your day and again at the end. As you do this, you're training your mind and body for future grief bursts that will come.

The more you practice, the more of a habit deep breathing will become and the easier you'll be able to initiate it when you need it.

Before you read on, practice deep breathing for a few more minutes.

Again, this simple skill can be massively beneficial during this time of mourning. And the good news is that anyone can do it, anytime, anywhere.

After the death of a sister or brother, the shock can be immense. Sometimes we can actually forget to breathe.

Taking care of yourself in this way is one way you can honor your sibling and love those around you.

Breathe.

9

"I THINK I'M ANGRY"

"I'm frustrated, confused, and upset. Actually, I think I'm angry."

– E.L.

Anger is a natural grief emotion. It comes to almost all grieving hearts.

Anger is common and sometimes intense when a sibling dies.

Anger is powerful. We see its negative effects in the world and in our own past. Many of us struggle with how to best handle it.

Anger is an emotion. As such, it is neutral. How we deal with and express our anger, however, can be either positive and healing or negative and hurtful.

Anger takes many forms. Upset and frustration. Impatience and irritability. Agitation and aggressive driving. Rages and explosions. Silence and depression. Unhealthy habits and addictions.

We're wired for connection. We're made to love and be loved. Siblings have unique relationships and special connections.

When a brother or sister dies, our hearts are broken. Though we know death happens, it feels wrong somehow. Anger is a natural result.

Acknowledging your anger is the first step. Finding healthy ways to express it and "let it out" will be important in your grief process.

When do you typically get angry?

_____

_____

_____

_____

_____

_____

_____

How do you usually express that anger?

_____

_____

_____

_____

_____

_____

_____

_____

Writing Prompts:

Use the following prompts to begin to process your grief anger. Be as honest as you can. Write whatever comes to mind:

"Since the death of my sibling, I've found myself angry about..."

_____

_____

_____

_____

_____

_____

_____

"When it comes to managing anger, I wish I could..."

_____

_____

_____

_____

_____

_____

_____

_____

Letter Writing Exercise

There are times when writing a letter can be extremely helpful and healing. In this case, consider writing a letter to someone you are angry with. Of course, this is a letter you will never send.

Picture the person in front of you. Yes, it might even be your deceased sibling. Write what you feel inside. Resist the temptation to hold back or censor yourself. The goal is to "get the anger out."

_____

_____

_____

_____

_____

_____

_____

_____

_____

_____

_____

_____

_____

_____

_____

_____

_____

_____

_____

_____

_____

_____

_____

_____

_____

_____

_____

_____

_____

_____

_____

_____

_____

The loss of a brother or sister is traumatic in many ways. Feeling angry is natural for the surviving sibling.

Managing grief anger is difficult. Be patient with yourself. Acknowledge the anger when it comes. Then focus on "getting it out" in healthy ways.

QUICK TIPS FOR HANDLING GRIEF ANGER

Practice the art of deep breathing. The more you make this a habit, the more beneficial it will be when anger rises within you. See yourself breathing in calm and breathing out your anger. See the end of chapter five for more info on this important grief processing skill.

- Exercise. Regular, moderate exercise appropriate for your age and health is extremely helpful in managing anger.

- Talk about your anger when it comes. Talk out loud to yourself when alone. Share and vent with someone safe who will just listen.

- Punch a pillow. Walk around punching the air.

- Scream and yell. Scream into a pillow. Yell in a private place where you won't be disturbed.

Once you've processed the anger, see yourself releasing it. Picture the anger in your hand and make a fist. When you're ready, open your hand and release that anger.

Imagine your anger is a balloon you're holding onto. After you express that anger and "get it out," see yourself releasing the balloon. See your anger drifting up and away from you.

Limit your exposure to unhelpful people and influences. You don't need extra challenges right now.

10

"I HAVE A LOT OF GUILT AND REGRET"

"I look back and wince. I have a lot of guilt and regret,
and I don't know what to do with them."

– R.G.

After a sibling dies, guilt often comes knocking.

We naturally go back and think about what we could or should have done. We wince at some of what we did or didn't say or do. Our imperfections, mistakes, and perceived failures begin to haunt us.

"What if..." and "If only..." scenarios play repeatedly in our minds and hearts.

Many grieving siblings find it helpful to make a distinction between guilt and regret.

Regret says, "I wish I had or hadn't..." and "If I had known what I know now, I would have..." We all have regrets. Regrets are natural and reasonable.

Guilt says, "It's my fault. I'm responsible for what happened. I caused this." Guilt is an accuser. It points its crooked finger at us and sneers, "You did this."

When it comes to your own heart, try distinguishing your regrets from guilt.

Regrets:

"With regard to my sibling's death, I wish I had..."

_____

_____

_____

_____

_____

_____

"With regard to my sibling and their death, I wish I hadn't..."

_____

_____

_____

_____

_____

_____

"If I had known then what I know now, I would have..."

_____

_____

_____

_____

_____

_____

Guilt:

"When I think of my sibling, I feel it's my fault that..."

_____

_____

_____

_____

_____

_____

_____

"When I feel guilty, I usually..."

_____

_____

_____

_____

_____

_____

_____

Most grieving siblings tussle with guilt at some point. For many, the battle with guilt is difficult and ongoing. Distinguishing between guilt and regret can be helpful.

Letter Writing Exercise

Write a letter to yourself from your sibling. What would they say to you about your regrets and feelings of guilt?

Don't overthink this. Just write.

_____

_____

_____

_____

_____

_____

_____

_____

_____

_____

_____

_____

_____

_____

_____

11

"I DON'T FEEL ANYTHING"

"I'm surprised. I don't feel anything. It's like I'm numb."

– W.M.

The loss of a sibling can be emotionally overwhelming.

None of us can handle the full weight of loss all the time. Just like an electric circuit, our hearts can get overloaded. Our feelers can temporarily shut down.

Most grieving siblings experience a sense of numbness from time to time in their grief journey. This is natural and even healthy. Numbness, though it can be disturbing and uncomfortable, can help protect our hearts and minds from damage. We need breaks from grief's grinding intensity.

As with other aspects of grief, acknowledging what's happening inside us is the first step to processing it.

If you have felt numb in your grief journey, describe what that was like:

_____

_____

_____

_____

_____

_____

_____

_____

When you feel numb, what do you typically do? How does this affect your life and routine?

_____

_____

_____

_____

_____

_____

_____

_____

Writing Prompts:

Use the following prompts to begin to process this emotional numbness. Write whatever comes to mind.

"When I'm numb (when I feel nothing), I wonder..."

_____

_____

_____

_____

_____

_____

"When I'm numb, I'm most concerned about..."

_____

_____

_____

_____

_____

_____

_____

Feeling numb is something experienced by many grieving siblings. Be kind to yourself. Accept yourself where you are, as you are.

12

"AM I DEPRESSED?"

"Since my sister died, it's like I've lost interest in the
world. I have no motivation. Am I depressed?"

– A.D.

———— ✦⟨⟩✦ ————

The emotional onslaught after a sibling's death can be heavy.

We experience sadness, frustration, anger, fear, anxiety, and guilt.
At times, we might feel nothing at all.

Our world has changed. Our family has changed forever. We are
changing.

We don't like this new life. All of this put together can be depressing.

Most grieving siblings experience some depression on their grief
journey. In most cases, this depression is temporary and situational. In
other words, most of us feel depressed for a period of time directly as
a result of sibling's death.

How do you know if you're depressed? Here are some typical
signs of temporary depression that grievers can experience:

- An ongoing sense of sadness

- Frequent bouts of crying

- Poor concentration

- Lack of motivation

- Loss of pleasure

- Withdrawing from usual or normal activities

- Loneliness and increased social isolation

- Hopelessness

Temporary, situational depression can come and go throughout the grief process.

Rather than hiding this, being intentional about processing this depression is crucial. We need to open the spillways of our grief reservoir and "let the depression out."

If you've felt depressed since the death of your sibling, describe what that was like. What did you feel, think, and experience?

_____

_____

_____

_____

_____

_____

_____

_____

_____

_____

_____

_____

_____

_____

When you're depressed, what do you think would be helpful to you?

_____

_____

_____

_____

_____

_____

_____

_____

_____

_____

_____

_____

_____

_____

_____

_____

_____

_____

Writing Prompts:

Use the prompts below to express more of your heart and mind regarding some of the grief depression you have experienced.

"Since my sibling died, I feel depressed when I think of…"

_____

_____

_____

_____

_____

_____

_____

_____

"When I feel depressed, I hope that…"

_____

_____

_____

_____

_____

_____

_____

_____

_____

Letter Writing Exercise

Write a letter to someone safe that you trust. You won't send this letter, of course, but having the recipient in mind will help you write. Think of a time that you felt depressed. Tell them about it. Don't limit yourself to this page. Feel free to use extra paper or write the letter in a separate notebook.

_____

_____

_____

_____

_____

_____

_____

_____

_____

_____

_____

_____

_____

_____

_____

_____

_____

_____

_____

_____

_____

_____

_____

_____

_____

_____

_____

_____

_____

Experiencing some temporary situational depression is common in the grief process. These heavy feelings and thoughts are natural during the sibling grief journey. Be kind to yourself.

For many of us, there are times when seeking professional input is helpful or even necessary. Please don't hesitate to reach out to a licensed counselor, grief professional, or grief coach.

PART TWO:
THE MENTAL CHALLENGES

Grief hits not only our hearts but also our minds. When
a sibling dies, the mental impact is significant.

Our thoughts spin. Our brains become foggy.

We can't focus or concentrate like usual. Memory issues
can surface. We can feel like we're losing our minds.

In this section, we're going to explore the
mental impact sibling loss can have.

Take your time as you move through these pages. Express what's
happening inside you. Be kind to yourself along the way.

13

"MY MIND IS SPINNING"

"My mind is spinning. I can't think straight.
My thoughts bounce all over the place."

– C.C.

———————◦◦◦◦———————

The loss of a sibling affects us mentally.

Our minds move with amazing speed. When we're grieving, our thoughts can bounce all over the place. Most grieving siblings experience their share of mental spinning.

We wonder about this or that. Concerns swirl around us. Our to-do list is a mile long. Our thoughts go round and round. Our brains feel like a hamster on a wheel. Our minds are moving, but our thoughts don't seem to be going anywhere.

Writing can be helpful here. Our hands (or fingers if we're typing) move much slower than our brains. When we write, we force our minds to slow down enough to express some of what's happening inside.

Writing gives our circling, bouncing thoughts a place to land.

Have you experienced some mental spinning since your sibling's death? Describe what this is like for you.

_____

_____

_____

_____

_____

_____

_____

_____

How do you usually respond when your mind spins?

_____

_____

_____

_____

_____

_____

_____

Writing Prompts:

Use the prompts below to help process your spinning thoughts. Free yourself to express wherever your mind takes you.

"Since my sibling died, my mind tends to spin about…"

_____

_____

_____

_____

_____

_____

_____

"When my mind spins, the thoughts that concern me the most are…"

_____

_____

_____

_____

_____

_____

_____

_____

Memory Writing Exercise

When your mind spins, what particular memories of your sibling surface? Briefly list some of those memories here:

_____

_____

_____

_____

_____

_____

_____

Pick one of these memories. Write about that memory below. Write whatever comes to mind. Let your heart express itself.

_____

_____

_____

_____

_____

_____

_____

_____

_____

_____

_____

_____

_____

_____

_____

_____

_____

_____

_____

_____

_____

_____

_____

_____

Mental spinning is natural and common for surviving siblings. Process this mental whirlwind as you can. Consider having a sheet of paper or notepad handy for these times. When your mind spins, try writing your thoughts.

Over time, "getting the grief out" in this way will be relieving and healing.

14

"MY BRAIN IS TIRED"

"My head is heavy. My brain is tired."

– J.T.

———— ✦ ————

Grief is exhausting. The aftermath of a sibling's death is mentally draining.

We said previously that our brains can feel like a hamster on a wheel. Our minds go, and go, and go. Thoughts circle around and bounce about. The speed and constancy of all this mental activity can be exhausting.

Mental fatigue is the natural result, and it is common in grief.

Some grieving siblings report that their heads feel heavy. Others talk about zoning out or having difficulty thinking. Some have trouble finding the right words in conversations. Still others feel robotic - like they're just going through the motions.

Many say something like, "My brain feels tired."

Have you experienced any of these things? If so, describe what mental fatigue is like for you.

_____

_____

_____

_____

_____

_____

_____

_____

When your brain feels tired, what do you typically do? Do you wish you could do something different? If so, what?

_____

_____

_____

_____

_____

_____

_____

_____

_____

Letter Writing Exercise:

Write a letter to your sibling. Describe your mental fatigue to them. What are you thinking and feeling during these times? Be as specific as you can. Let your mind go. Write whatever comes.

_____

_____

_____

_____

_____

_____

_____

_____

_____

_____

_____

_____

_____

_____

_____

_____

_____

_____

_____

_____

_____

_____

_____

_____

_____

_____

_____

_____

_____

_____

_____

Brain fatigue is natural and common on the grief journey. When you write, you give your worn synapses a place to rest. Writing can be a form of exercise that helps "get the fatigue out."

15

"I CAN'T SEEM TO CONCENTRATE"

"I'm having trouble focusing. I can't seem
to concentrate. Is this grief?"

– G.J.

———◦◦◦———

After the death of a sibling, grief begins to gobble up our internal real estate. Grief thoughts and emotions surface and flood our systems.

Naturally, our ability to focus and concentrate will be affected.

We're not as quick or sharp mentally. We find our minds wandering more than usual. We tire more easily. We're not as resilient. We miss details. We neglect certain things without even realizing it. We make more mistakes.

Of course, this affects our work performance. We might be able to fake it for a while, but eventually it becomes clear we're not at our best right now. If others are depending on us and how well we perform, this adds additional stress to our already heavy load.

Many grieving siblings feel like they're "not all there." The reality is that grief is taking up a lot of our internal space. There is simply less mental energy left to do life right now.

Have you had more trouble focusing and concentrating since your sibling died? Do you sense your work is being affected? Describe what this has been like for you:

_____

_____

_____

_____

_____

_____

_____

_____

When we have difficulty focusing, many of us are hard on ourselves. When you notice you're having trouble concentrating, what do you say to yourself? Is what you say to yourself helpful?

_____

_____

_____

_____

_____

_____

_____

_____

Writing Prompts:

Use the prompts below to write about this issue. Resist the temptation to over-analyze. Just write whatever comes to mind.

"Since my sibling's death, I notice I have trouble concentrating when..."

_____

_____

_____

_____

_____

_____

_____

_____

"When I have trouble focusing, I tend to..."

_____

_____

_____

_____

_____

_____

_____

"I think it might help if I..."

_____

_____

_____

_____

_____

_____

_____

_____

_____

_____

_____

_____

_____

_____

_____

_____

_____

_____

_____

_____

Poetry Writing Exercise:

Using the following list of words, try writing a poem about the focus and concentration issues you've faced since your sibling died. Feel free to use any other words you wish in addition to these. Don't be concerned about rhyme, meter, or composition. Free yourself to use these words to express what you think and feel.

*Heart   Mind   Brain   Focus   Concentrate   Wander
Wonder   Think   Head   Thoughts   Trouble*

_____

_____

_____

_____

_____

_____

_____

_____

_____

_____

_____

_____

_____

_____

_____

_____

_____

_____

_____

_____

_____

_____

_____

_____

_____

_____

_____

_____

_____

_____

Most surviving siblings experience concentration issues on their grief journey. Your brain is being squeezed by grief. As you process your grief in healthy ways, your mental focus will likely return. Be patient. Do what you can to accept yourself along the way.

16

"MY MEMORY HAS GOTTEN MUCH WORSE"

"My memory is terrible. Since my brother's death,
my memory has gotten much worse."

– R.H.

"My memory is much worse now" is a common statement among those on the grief journey. Memory issues are often part of the sibling grief journey.

We can't remember where we put things. We forget why we came into the room. We blip out in the middle of a sentence. We can't seem to find the right words. We miss appointments. We can't recall what we did last week, yesterday, or even an hour ago.

These brain blips can be disconcerting. We wonder what's happening.

Is something wrong? Are we developing Dementia? Do we have a tumor? Are we going crazy?

The death of our sibling and the resulting grief have upset our usual balance. We have less available mental space right now. We're mentally overcrowded. Our brains can't hold it all.

Increased forgetfulness is natural, reasonable, and common in the grief process.

Are you more forgetful since your sibling's death? Write about this. Give some examples.

_____

_____

_____

_____

_____

_____

_____

_____

When you realize you've forgotten something, how do you react?

_____

_____

_____

_____

_____

_____

_____

_____

_____

Writing Prompts:

New or increased memory problems can be frustrating and unnerving. Use the prompts below to process this.

"When I forget something, I wonder (or worry) about..."

_____

_____

_____

_____

_____

_____

_____

_____

_____

_____

_____

_____

_____

_____

_____

_____

"With regard to my memory, I think I could help myself by..."

_____

_____

_____

_____

_____

_____

_____

_____

_____

_____

_____

_____

_____

The loss of a sibling hits our entire being, including our minds. Amid the whirlwind of emotion and change, it's natural for some thoughts to get lost along the way.

You're not superhuman. You're hurting and grieving. Give yourself a break.

As you continue to process your sibling grief in healthy ways, your memory will likely bounce back over time.

17

"AM I GOING CRAZY?"

"I'm not myself. I feel confused sometimes.
I can't seem to remember anything.

Am I going crazy?"

– B.T.

———————

When a sibling dies, our families and personal worlds are permanently altered. In some sense, everything is different now.

We look around us, however, and everything looks much the same.

The rest of the world zips along much as before. It's like we're living in some alternate reality looking in from the outside. Weird. Surreal. This is frustrating and confusing.

Feeling confused or even a little crazy is common for those on the sibling grief journey.

We're not crazy, but life seems crazy now compared to before. It's like someone rearranged everything overnight. We woke up in a different world. Nothing feels the same.

Our hearts and minds are desperately trying to make sense of all this. Feeling a bit unhinged every now and then is a natural result.

Have you felt a little crazy since your sibling died? Describe some examples:

_____

_____

_____

_____

_____

_____

_____

_____

When you're feeling a little crazy, what do you typically do? What do you sense you're telling yourself? Is it helpful?

_____

_____

_____

_____

_____

_____

_____

_____

_____

Letter Writing Exercise

Imagine yourself to be a detached observer watching you on your grief journey. Write yourself a letter from this perspective. What would a detached, outside observer say to you about "feeling crazy" after your sibling's death?

Again, don't overthink this. Write whatever comes to mind. Resist the temptation to edit as you go. Just write.

_____

_____

_____

_____

_____

_____

_____

_____

_____

_____

_____

_____

_____

_____

_____

_____

_____

_____

_____

_____

_____

_____

_____

_____

_____

_____

_____

_____

_____

_____

_____

Feeling a little unhinged is common for grieving siblings. The overwhelming amount of change that flows from your sibling's passing can be staggering.

Breathe deeply. You're not crazy, but loss and the resulting grief can make you wonder.

PART THREE:
THE PHYSICAL IMPACT

When we lose a sibling, our bodies feel the shock.

We can begin to experience weird or exacerbated symptoms and more frequent illnesses.

The constant stress of all the change occurring in our lives can whittle away at our health.

The daily grind of grief can wear us out.

In this section, we'll delve into the frustrating and often disturbing physical impact grief can have.

18

"I FEEL LIKE MY BODY IS FALLING APART!"

"I don't know what's happening. One physical trouble
after another. I feel like my body is falling apart."

– H.E.

The loss of a sibling hits our entire being. Our bodies feel the shock
too.

As a result, many on the sibling grief journey experience new or
exacerbated symptoms.

Headaches, migraines, muscle tension, joint pain, and back pain.
Stomach distress, gastrointestinal issues, nausea, dizziness, and ver-
tigo. Racing heartbeat, palpitations, chest pressure, chest pain, arrhyth-
mias, and shortness of breath. Fatigue, exhaustion, insomnia, colds,
flu, illnesses, and infections.

The list goes on and on.

The death of a sibling can have stunning physical impact. Our
health can wobble and shake under the ongoing weight of grief. Taking
care of ourselves becomes more important than ever.

Some symptoms can be worrisome and frightening. If we're
concerned, we need to reach to a medical professional. Amid all this
upheaval, we need to know we're okay. Reassurance is priceless when
we're grieving.

Have you experienced any new or exacerbated symptoms or health issues since your sibling died? If so, list them here.

_____

_____

_____

_____

_____

_____

_____

When you experience these physical issues, how does it affect your daily life?

_____

_____

_____

_____

_____

_____

_____

_____

_____

Writing Prompts:

Use the following prompts to process what's happening to you physically. Let your mind go where it wants to. Write freely.

"When I think of the symptoms I'm experiencing (or have experienced) since my sibling's death, I wonder about..."

_____

_____

_____

_____

_____

_____

_____

"Amid all the stress and change, I could take better care of myself by..."

_____

_____

_____

_____

_____

_____

_____

Poetry Writing Exercise:

Using the following words, try writing a poem about the symptoms you've experienced since your sibling's death. Don't be overly concerned about whether your poem rhymes or what it looks like. Let your heart express what's happening inside you.

Heart   Body   Sibling   Afraid   Strange   Pain
Grief   Loss   Time   Health

_____

_____

_____

_____

_____

_____

_____

_____

_____

_____

_____

_____

_____

_____

_____

_____

_____

_____

_____

_____

_____

_____

_____

_____

_____

_____

_____

_____

_____

_____

_____

_____

_____

Many grieving siblings encounter frustrating and troubling physical symptoms. Breathe deeply. If needed, reach out to your physician for reassurance and input. Do what you can to take good care of yourself.

19

"I'M EXHAUSTED"

"I'm tired all the time now. I'm exhausted."

– T.A.

The number one physical symptom reported by those in sibling grief is fatigue.

Loss hits. Grief invades. Emotions go wacky. Our minds spin and bounce. Managing all the change is draining.

Grief saps our strength. Our capacities are stretched and squeezed. Our worlds have been altered, and yet our responsibilities have not diminished. We're stunned, but life moves on and drags us along with it.

Exhaustion is commonplace. As one griever said, "Even chewing my food takes herculean effort."

Life is demanding and busy. Most of us are tired most of the time. The loss of our sibling and the resulting grief can rocket our fatigue to new heights.

Just getting through the day is a huge accomplishment.

Describe the fatigue you've experienced since your sibling died. Be as detailed as possible.

_____

_____

_____

_____

_____

_____

_____

When fatigue hits, what do you wish you could do?

_____

_____

_____

_____

_____

_____

_____

_____

_____

_____

Writing Prompts:

Use the following prompts to write more about grief exhaustion.

"When fatigue hits me, some of the things that are not helpful to me are..."

_____

_____

_____

_____

_____

"When I'm exhausted, some things I can do to take care of myself are..."

_____

_____

_____

_____

_____

_____

Fatigue and even exhaustion are common in sibling grief. Your body is feeling the weight of this terrible loss. Something huge has happened.

Breathe deeply. Accept yourself as you are. Do what you can to express your grief in healthy ways.

20

"I'M NOT SLEEPING WELL"

"I can't seem to rest. I'm not sleeping well.
It's almost like I'm too tired to sleep."

– S.D.

———————

Most grieving siblings struggle with sleep disturbances of some kind.

Our lives have been upended. Our families have been altered. Our emotions, thoughts, and bodies are being shaken. It makes sense that our sleep would be disturbed too.

We have trouble getting to sleep. In the quiet of the night, our minds kick into high gear. We replay the past. We wonder and worry. Emotions surge up within us.

We have trouble staying asleep. We toss and turn. Perhaps we have dreams of our loved one - or even nightmares. We wake up trembling.

We wake up tired. Our minds and hearts work all night long. We can wonder if we really slept at all.

It's been said that sleep deprivation is the most basic form of torture. We heal when we sleep. Good rest is essential to good health. At a time when we need it the most, restful sleep seems to elude us.

How has your sleep been since your sibling's death? What changes have you experienced that are different from your norm?

_____

_____

_____

_____

_____

_____

_____

Describe a typical night from the time you go to bed until you get up:

_____

_____

_____

_____

_____

_____

_____

_____

Writing Prompts:

Use the following prompts to process this more.

"Since my sibling died, when I go to bed, I find myself thinking and feeling..."

_____

_____

_____

_____

_____

_____

_____

_____

"With regard to my sleep, I wish I could..."

_____

_____

_____

_____

_____

_____

_____

"Things that might help my sleep are…"

_____

_____

_____

_____

_____

_____

_____

_____

_____

_____

_____

_____

_____

_____

_____

_____

_____

Memory Writing Exercise:

When your mind is spinning at night and you can't sleep, are there certain memories of your sibling that surface repeatedly? List these repetitive thoughts below:

_____

_____

_____

_____

_____

_____

_____

Pick one memory of the memories above. Write about this memory below. Express what's happening in your mind and heart.

_____

_____

_____

_____

_____

_____

_____

_____

_____

_____

_____

_____

_____

_____

_____

_____

_____

_____

_____

_____

_____

_____

_____

Altered sleep patterns are a common result of sibling loss. As you continue to process your grief for your sister or brother in healthy ways, your sleep will likely improve over time.

Now is not forever. Be kind to yourself. Do what you can to promote better rest during this time.

21

"I DON'T HAVE AN APPETITE ANYMORE"

"I've been losing weight since my sister died.
I don't have an appetite anymore."

– J.M.

When a sibling dies, if affects every part of our lives. This includes how we eat.

Grief tends to dull the senses. Food doesn't taste the same now. Many don't feel hungry and forget to eat. Some don't feel thirsty and don't hydrate well. Our clothes feel loose and baggy. We lose weight.

Others eat for comfort. We might be drawn to carbs and sugar. If we did this before, we might do this even more while grieving. We gain weight and feel even worse.

We need good nutrition now more than ever. Yet eating well tends to be a challenge. Healthy eating often takes more effort, planning, and preparation. The more grief squeezes us, the more we opt for the easy and convenient.

Eating well is challenging in our busy world. We have to make intentional, ongoing choices to pursue personal wellness. When grieving, these choices can be even more difficult.

Have you noticed changes in your eating habits since your sibling died? Describe them.

_____

_____

_____

_____

_____

_____

_____

On a scale of 1 to 10, with 10 being the best, how would you rate your nutritional intake and eating habits? Describe why you chose this number.

_____

_____

_____

_____

_____

_____

_____

Writing Prompts:

Use these prompts to process this issue of eating and nutrition a bit more. Don't hold back. Write whatever comes to mind.

"When it comes to food and nutrition right now, I feel..."

_____

_____

_____

_____

_____

_____

_____

"When it comes to food and nutrition, I would like to be able to..."

_____

_____

_____

_____

_____

_____

_____

_____

"When I'm ready, some small steps I could take toward greater wellness is..."

_____

_____

_____

_____

_____

_____

_____

"Recognizing that I'm stressed and grieving, I can be more patient with myself in all this by..."

_____

_____

_____

_____

_____

_____

_____

The loss of a sibling can greatly affect your appetite and eating habits. Be kind to yourself. As you see things you sense need to change, make small adjustments. The sibling grief journey can only be taken one step at a time.

22

"WHEN DID I BECOME SO ACCIDENT-PRONE?"

"Lately, if it can happen, it will happen to me.
When did I become so accident-prone?"

– P.A.

<hr>

After the loss of a sibling, we can become more accident-prone.

We stumble. We trip over our own feet. We bump into things and people. We cut ourselves while shaving or chopping vegetables. We burn ourselves while cooking. We shut our fingers in doors. We get injured more easily.

We drop things. We spill drinks and food. We drive differently. We can't seem to park straight. Our depth perception is off. Our balance is not what it was.

Many grieving siblings experience balance and coordination issues. We naturally wonder if something is wrong. This can be incredibly frustrating.

If we're concerned, the best thing is to consult our physician. A little reassurance can be comforting. We're dealing with enough uncertainty as it is.

Most of the time, our coordination and balance troubles will be short-lived. As we process our grief in healthy ways, our current clumsiness will likely recede into the background over time.

Have you been more accident-prone since your sibling died? Describe this:

_____

_____

_____

_____

_____

_____

_____

Is there anything you sense you can do to reduce accidents and injuries on your grief journey? Try to list a few things:

_____

_____

_____

_____

_____

_____

_____

_____

Writing Prompts:

Use the following prompts to think more about balance or coordination challenges.

"When I have an accident of some kind, I feel..."

_____

_____

_____

_____

_____

_____

"While grieving and being more accident-prone, I can be kind to myself by..."

_____

_____

_____

_____

_____

Sibling grief expresses itself in many ways, including coordination and balance. Slowing down a bit may help. Accepting ourselves along the way is important.

The world is not easy on grieving hearts. We need to give ourselves mercy, grace, and a lot of kindness.

23

"THE STRESS IS MAKING ME SICK"

"The stress is making me sick. The grief
is grinding and relentless."

– M.M.

———————◦◇◦———————

Loss is a natural stress-producer.

The grief process for siblings is packed with change. Change, even good change, is stressful. We lived stressful lives before. Now, the grinding pressure of grief stress can feel unrelenting.

Over time, stress suppresses our immune systems. Many grieving siblings report more frequent colds and illnesses. Issues that our bodies were able to keep in check before may begin to surface. Some can even develop stress-related diseases as a result of all the upheaval.

Can grief make a person sick? Yes, it can.

Again, checking in with our physician during a time of loss is important. We need their care, reassurance, and guidance.

Reducing our stress is crucial. We tend to be hard on ourselves. We don't need that kind of pressure when we're already down. Taking care of ourselves needs to be a priority.

Has your stress level increased since your sibling's death? How so?

_____

_____

_____

_____

_____

_____

_____

_____

How does your grief stress seem to show itself physically?

_____

_____

_____

_____

_____

_____

_____

_____

Letter Writing Exercise

Become a detached observer of yourself. See yourself under all the weight of this grief stress. Notice how it's affecting you.

Write a letter to yourself. Consider the following things as topics in your letter:

- How you see grief stress affecting your life.

- What you would say to yourself to express concern, kindness, and hope.

- What you would tell yourself to do that might help.

_____

_____

_____

_____

_____

_____

_____

_____

_____

_____

_____

_____

_____

_____

_____

_____

_____

_____

_____

_____

_____

_____

_____

_____

_____

_____

_____

_____

_____

_____

_____

Write freely. Resist the temptation to edit. Write whatever comes to mind.

Sibling grief is incredibly stressful. Reduce what stress you can. Make self-care a priority.

24

"MY DREAMS HAVE BEEN CRAZY"

"Since my sister died, my dreams have been crazy.
I guess there's more happening inside me that I thought."

– S.L.

During our sleep, we tend to process things our minds can't get to during the day. Our subconscious mind is always awake. Our dreams and nightmares are often a reflection of this.

As grieving siblings, there's more happening inside us than we're aware of. When we sleep, many of these subconscious things bubble up to the surface. Just as sleep can promote physical healing, it can also give us a needed opportunity to process what we can't when we're awake.

Many have dreams about their departed sisters and brothers. Some dreams may be reassuring. Others may cause us to question this or that. Some dreams bring joy, while others stir our longings.

Some surviving siblings have nightmares along the way. These are often related to traumatic events and mental images (real or imagined). If we feel personally responsible for some aspect of our sibling's death, this weighs heavily on us and can express itself during our sleep.

Not everyone has dreams of their sibling. This can be disturbing to some. We can feel like we've forgotten them somehow. We can end up thinking there's something wrong with us.

If we have dreams or nightmares, processing them well is important.

Have you had dreams and / or nightmares since your sibling's death? If so, describe what they are typically like. If you haven't had any dreams, describe how you feel about this:

_____

_____

_____

_____

_____

_____

_____

_____

_____

_____

_____

_____

_____

_____

If you could write your own script for a dream, what would it include?

_____

_____

_____

Writing Prompts:

Try processing your dreams and / or nightmares further by using these prompts.

"Since my sibling died, one dream (or nightmare) I particularly remember is..." (If you don't have dreams, try this prompt: "I wish I could have a dream where..."):

_____

_____

_____

_____

_____

_____

_____

"After a dream (or nightmare) with my sibling in it, I find myself wondering..." (or "What concerns me about not having dreams about my sibling is…"):

_____

_____

_____

_____

_____

_____

_____

Poetry Writing Exercise:

Try writing a poem about your dreams using the words below. Free yourself to express what you think and feel.

Dream   Sleep   Awake   Remember   Heart
Mind   Wonder   Grief   Sibling

_____

_____

_____

_____

_____

_____

_____

_____

_____

_____

_____

_____

_____

_____

_____

_____

_____

_____

_____

_____

_____

_____

_____

_____

_____

_____

_____

_____

_____

_____

_____

_____

Our subconscious mind is always active. Dreams or nightmares about our sibling can be common. Continue to process these as they come.

25

"I MUST TAKE BETTER CARE OF MYSELF"

"This is harder than I would have ever dreamed.
I must take better care of myself."

– B.H.

Self-care is always a priority. While grieving the loss of a sister or brother, taking good care of ourselves is even more imperative.

In times of heavy stress, self-care is often neglected. After a sibling's death, we marshal our energies toward getting things done and fulfilling our responsibilities. Life requires even more energy and effort than it did before.

We find ourselves in a quandary. Self-care puts gas back in our tank, but it feels like there's not enough in our tank to pursue adequate self-care.

Good self-care is always a choice. As such, we must choose pursuing personal wellness over something else. We need to resist constantly giving way to the tyranny of the urgent. We need to put (and keep) first things first.

A great gift we can give to those around us is the healthiest us possible. This benefits everyone. This also honors our sibling. Making self-care a priority is one way of saying "I love you" to both our sibling and those around us.

How has the loss of your sibling impacted your self-care? Describe this.

_____

_____

_____

_____

_____

_____

_____

_____

When you think of self-care, what kinds of things come to mind? List them.

_____

_____

_____

_____

_____

_____

_____

_____

_____

Writing Prompts:

Use these prompts to process more about self-care and pursing personal wellness while grieving.

"When it comes to self-care, I tend to be pretty good at..."

_____

_____

_____

_____

_____

_____

_____

"When it comes to taking care of myself, I tend to struggle with..."

_____

_____

_____

_____

_____

_____

_____

_____

"I believe that good self-care is important because..."

_____

_____

_____

_____

_____

_____

_____

"When it comes to taking care of myself and pursuing personal wellness, I think my next step is..." (and describe how you would do this).

_____

_____

_____

_____

_____

_____

_____

_____

_____

_____

_____

_____

_____

_____

_____

_____

_____

_____

_____

_____

_____

_____

_____

_____

_____

Nutrition, hydration, exercise, and rest play big roles in personal wellness. Getting around safe, healthy people and limiting your exposure to unhelpful influences is also important.

Self-care, like everything else on the sibling grief road, is a journey that we can only take one step at a time.

You are unique in human history. There's never been another person exactly like you, even if you're a twin. You matter deeply. We need you.

PART FOUR:
THE SPIRITUAL SHAKING

In the previous sections, you processed how your sibling's
death has affected you emotionally, mentally, and physically.

In this section, you'll be exploring the
spiritual impact of this heavy loss.

We're relational beings at our core. When a sister
or brother departs, our souls can shake.

Perhaps we begin to question things we were sure about before.

Maybe we experience new doubts, fears, or even a faith crisis.

We end up living out what we really believe deep
inside. Taking our souls seriously in the grief process
is crucial to good self-care and to healing.

26
"I HAVE SO MANY QUESTIONS"

"I just can't fathom this. Maybe I'm still in
shock. I have so many questions."

– J.K.

When a sibling dies, our hearts are shaken. Soon, questions begin to surface. Many of these questions have spiritual roots to them.

"How did this happen? How *could* this happen?"

"What do I do? How do I handle this?"

"What's next? What does this mean for me?"

"Who is responsible for this? Couldn't someone have done something to change or prevent this?"

"Where was God? How does He fit into all this?"

"If things like this happen, what's it all for? What's the meaning of life anyway?"

Some questions might be disturbing to us. Other questions may have no answers. Yet our hearts must ask, and ask, and ask. Our hearts are squirming under the pain of our sibling's passing.

As with the rest of the sibling grief process, expressing what's happening inside us is helpful, relieving, and healing over time. We need to "get it out." Our soul questions need to be expressed.

What questions have surfaced in your mind and heart since your sibling's death? List them here.

_____

_____

_____

_____

_____

_____

_____

_____

_____

_____

_____

_____

_____

_____

_____

_____

Writing Prompts:

Use these prompts to process these questions further. Don't hold back or censor yourself. Write freely whatever comes to your mind and heart.

"Of all the questions that have surfaced, the ones I find myself asking over and over are..."

_____

_____

_____

_____

_____

_____

"If I had to describe what my heart and soul are saying through these questions, I would say..."

_____

_____

_____

_____

_____

_____

Being aware of and expressing your heart-soul questions is an important part of your grief process. These wonderings run deep. Letting them surface, getting them out, and accepting yourself along the way will be helpful.

27

"WHY?"

"All my questions seem to begin with
'Why'. Why him? Why now?

Why that way? Why us? Why?"

– T.E.

The loss of a sibling can create all kinds of questions.

Of all the questions running around in our hearts and souls, "Why?" tends to be the deepest and most perplexing.

"Why did this happen? Why them? Why me? Why us? Why this way? Why now? Why?"

For most why questions, however, answers are hard to come by.

We're not perfect. We can't know everything. We're not in control. We're very limited. Even if we knew the answer to our why questions, would it be emotionally satisfying?

Chances are, no matter what answer we come up with, it will feel hollow. The reality is that our sibling is gone from our sight. We want them back. We wish they were still here. We're hurting.

Though we get no satisfying answers, our why questions are important. We must express them. As we air these questions, we can begin to process the thoughts and emotions behind them.

This leads to healing, adjustment, recovery, and growth over time.

What kind of why questions has your heart and soul been asking? List them here. Be as specific as possible.

_____

_____

_____

_____

_____

_____

_____

When you look at your questions above, describe how you feel. Write what's happening inside you, as best you can.

_____

_____

_____

_____

_____

_____

_____

_____

Writing Prompts:

Use these prompts to process your why questions further. Try not to edit in your mind as you go. Write freely.

"My biggest why question seems to be..." (after writing that question, continue to express where your heart and soul go next).

_____

_____

_____

_____

_____

_____

_____

"With regard to my biggest why question, I think it might help if I..."

_____

_____

_____

_____

_____

_____

_____

_____

Poetry Writing Exercise:

Using the following list of words to spur you on, try writing a poem that expresses some of your why questions. Don't worry about rhyme or composition. Express your heart and soul.

Heart   *Soul*   *Why*   *God*   *Questions*   *Pain*
Grief   *Heal*   *Afraid*   *Remember*

_____

_____

_____

_____

_____

_____

_____

_____

_____

_____

_____

_____

_____

_____

_____

_____

_____

_____

_____

_____

_____

_____

_____

_____

_____

_____

_____

_____

_____

_____

"Why?" is a natural and common question for surviving siblings. Keep expressing your why questions as they come. Get them out. Process them as best you can.

Be patient with yourself. Accept yourself as you are, as best you can.

28

"I'M MAD AT GOD"

"I'm upset. I'm angry. And I'm mad at God."

– P.B.

———————

In this grief process, many surviving siblings find themselves angry with God at some point.

Anger looks for a target. We naturally search for who or what is responsible for our sibling's death.

We have various targets available. We might blame other people such as family or friends that caused our sibling stress. We could see medical professionals or the people around our sister or brother at the end as being responsible somehow.

Our anger might become focused on things or situations like cancer, heart disease, a flawed medical system, a stressful job, poor safety protocols, natural disasters, or war.

Once the blaming begins, many of us eventually turn our anger on God. After all, we reason, the buck stops with Him.

"Why did God allow this?"

"Why didn't He do something to stop this?"

"Did God do this? Why?"

"Why did God take them from me?"

Whatever our questions, our souls need to express them outwardly. We need to "get the questions out," as many times as necessary. If we're angry at God, we need to find healthy ways to express it.

"But it's not okay to be angry with God!" some might say.

Even if we think this, it doesn't change the fact that we are angry with Him. And if He is God, He knows this already. We can't hide from Him or from ourselves. Good relationships thrive on trust. Part of trust is being willing to share what's happening inside us with the other party.

Even if you don't believe in God, you can still find yourself angry at Him. This is not unusual. Like other grief emotions, "getting it out" is key to the healing process.

When you think about your sibling's death, what questions do you have for God? List them here:

_____

_____

_____

_____

_____

_____

_____

If you've been upset or angry with God since your sibling's passing, begin to write about this below. Write whatever comes to mind.

_____

_____

_____

_____

_____

Letter Writing Exercise:

Write a letter to God expressing what you're thinking and feeling about Him and your loss. Tell Him what you're angry about. Express your angst and frustration to Him. Get it out.

_____

_____

_____

_____

_____

_____

_____

_____

_____

_____

_____

_____

_____

_____

_____

_____

Being angry with God at some point in the grief process is common. Don't keep this inside. Get it out. Get the anger out in healthy ways. If He is God, He already knows. He can handle your anger.

29

"EVEN OTHER PEOPLE OF FAITH DON'T GET IT"

"I expected more support from my church.
Even other people of faith don't get it."

– J.D.

The death of a sibling can shake us spiritually - and this includes our relationships with those of like faith.

We expect people of similar faith to be compassionate and supportive. Most of them are, at least for a little while. However, some will probably disappoint us.

They will say unhelpful things. They might spout spiritual platitudes and clichés at us rather than listening. They might not know how to be supportive, so they distance themselves from us. Perhaps they ignore us all together. Maybe they try to fix us and our loss somehow.

When these things happen, we naturally feel misunderstood, belittled, or even rejected.

People don't deal well with pain and grief, even people of faith. Most people tend to run when they feel uncomfortable. They feel insecure and out-of-control. Perhaps our grief triggers theirs, and they simply don't want to go into the pain again.

Whatever the reason, lack of support from people of like faith can be confusing, frustrating, and angering. Processing these disappointments is crucial for the health of hearts and souls.

Have people of similar faith disappointed you since your sibling's passing? Describe some of this:

_____

_____

_____

_____

_____

_____

_____

Specifically, what have people said and done that has shocked, confused, or frustrated you?

_____

_____

_____

_____

_____

_____

_____

_____

_____

Letter Writing Exercise:

Write a letter to those of similar faith who have disappointed you since your sibling's death. Tell them how you feel about what they said and did. Tell them what you wish they had done or said instead. Don't overthink this. Write whatever comes to mind.

_____

_____

_____

_____

_____

_____

_____

_____

_____

_____

_____

_____

_____

_____

_____

_____

_____

_____

_____

_____

_____

_____

_____

_____

_____

_____

_____

_____

_____

_____

_____

After the loss of a sibling, there's no guarantee that those of like faith will understand or be supportive. Lowering our expectations and processing painful interactions are important.

30

"I FEEL LIKE I'M HAVING A FAITH CRISIS"

"This has shaken me to the core. I feel
like I'm having a faith crisis."

– B.N.

Sibling loss can shake the soul.

What we believe can come under some intense examination. Perhaps we now doubt some things we were sure of. Maybe we become sure of some things that we doubted. Most of us wonder about how all this fits together.

Spiritual questioning is common in the sibling grief process. Doubts about various things surface in many grieving hearts. Being honest with ourselves and letting our hearts express these things is key to our healing and growth.

We can begin to process questions and doubts by acknowledging and identifying them. Once identified, we can talk and write about them. As with all aspects of sibling grief, expressing what's happening inside us is crucial.

This loss can lead some surviving siblings into a faith crisis where most of what they believed before is called into question. Acknowledging and processing this is essential, though it might be scary. Some of the best things in life are unnerving and hard.

Are there things that you believed before your sibling's death that you now doubt or wonder about? List those things here:

_____

_____

_____

_____

_____

_____

_____

_____

Is there someone you consider to be a spiritual mentor of sorts? Do you sense you could share with them some of what's happening inside you? What do you think might be the benefit of this?

_____

_____

_____

_____

_____

_____

_____

_____

Writing Prompts:

Use the following prompts to dig deeper into this topic. Write freely. Try not to censor yourself. Get it out.

"Since my sibling's death, the thoughts and doubts that are the most disturbing to me are..."

_____

_____

_____

_____

_____

_____

_____

"When I think about these questions and doubts, I'm afraid that..."

_____

_____

_____

_____

_____

_____

_____

Memory Writing Exercise:

When you think about some of the questions and doubts you have, what memories of your sibling come to mind?

_____

_____

_____

_____

_____

_____

_____

Pick one of these memories and write about it below. Let your heart express itself.

_____

_____

_____

_____

_____

_____

_____

_____

_____

_____

_____

_____

_____

_____

_____

_____

_____

_____

_____

_____

_____

_____

_____

_____

As with other parts of the grief process, please don't attempt to do this alone. Connect with someone you trust who will listen well and walk with you in this.

Try not to look too far down the road. Stay in the now as much as possible by being honest about and processing what is. As you do this, your next steps will become clearer with time.

31

"MY SOUL IS TIRED"

"I'm exhausted, inside and out. Even my soul is tired."

– S.B.

Sibling loss and the resulting grief can be exhausting emotionally, physically, and spiritually. Even our souls can become weary.

When we are spiritually fatigued, we can become numb. We zone out spiritually. We can feel empty, listless, and even lifeless.

Spiritual numbness can be disturbing. It feels like we've entered an unknown wilderness. We're trying to trudge forward, but every step seems to take massive energy and effort. The colors of life have dimmed. Everything seems dull and drab.

Reminding ourselves that now is not forever is important. Things will change. As we accept ourselves where we are and process our grief well, we will heal over time.

Connecting with a trusted spiritual mentor can be encouraging and help give us perspective. We all need safe people we respect that we can share with. If we don't have such a person in our lives, we can ask ourselves who might fill this role.

Many grieving siblings experience spiritual fatigue and numbness. This is common and natural. Acknowledging what's happening and "getting it out" can be helpful and relieving.

Are you experiencing spiritual fatigue or numbness in your grief journey? (Or have you in the past?). Describe what this is like.

_____

_____

_____

_____

_____

_____

_____

_____

When you are spiritually exhausted or numb, how do you feel about yourself?

_____

_____

_____

_____

_____

_____

_____

_____

_____

_____

Writing Prompts:

Use these prompts to explore this more. As you write, let your heart go where it wants to. Record whatever comes to mind.

"When I think of myself spiritually, I'm most concerned that..."

_____

_____

_____

_____

_____

_____

_____

_____

"When it comes to feeling spiritually exhausted and numb, I hope that..."

_____

_____

_____

_____

_____

_____

_____

Poetry Writing Exercise

Think about spiritual fatigue and numbness for a moment. What words come to mind. Make a list of these words here:

_____

_____

_____

_____

_____

_____

_____

Using the above words, write a brief poem. Don't worry about rhyme, meter, or format.

_____

_____

_____

_____

_____

_____

_____

_____

_____

_____

_____

_____

_____

_____

_____

_____

_____

_____

_____

_____

_____

_____

_____

_____

_____

_____

_____

_____

_____

_____

Spirituality and faith run deep and tend to be emotionally charged. Feeling empty or numb spiritually can be disconcerting and even frightening. Take your heart and soul seriously. Process what's happening inside you.

32

"I'VE GROWN SPIRITUALLY THROUGH THIS"

"This has been difficult beyond belief. I've learned a lot.
I've grown spiritually through this."

–R.J.

Many grieving siblings report that times of loss can be times of great spiritual growth. Loss and grief can teach us many lessons. Some of these lessons are life-changing.

We all want to live from our hearts. We want to love and be loved. We want to live with meaning and purpose. We want our days to count toward something greater than ourselves.

Sibling loss teaches us that almost anything can happen to anyone at any time. On the one hand, that can be terrifying. It can also be incredibly freeing. We discover what really matters to us. We can begin to live more in the moment and focus on taking one step at a time.

The loss of a brother or sister can lead us to look deeply into our own hearts and souls. If we're willing, we can honor our departed siblings by living with more meaning and purpose than ever before.

Much of life is about overcoming. Spiritual growth is possible during times of deep emotional pain and traumatic loss. This can be part of our healing process.

When you think about spiritual growth, what kind of things come to mind? What does spiritual growth look like to you?

How would you describe where you are spiritually at present?

Below is a portion of the Serenity Prayer by Reinhold Niebuhr. Read through it several times.

"God, grant me the grace to accept with serenity the things that cannot be changed,

The courage to change the things that should be changed,

And the wisdom to distinguish the one from the other.

Living one day at time,

Enjoying one moment at a time,

Accepting hardship as a pathway to peace."

What strikes you about this portion of Niebuhr's prayer? Write and express what happens inside you as you read it.

Write your own prayer. Don't overthink this. Focus on honestly expressing your heart. Even if you don't believe in God, try this, and see where it takes you.

Spirituality is a huge part of life. Many surviving siblings experience great spiritual growth during this season of loss. As you process your grief well, spiritual growth is possible for you as well.

In case you're interested, here is the entire Serenity Prayer.

"God, grant me the grace to accept with seren-
ity the things that cannot be changed,
The courage to change the things that should be changed,
And the wisdom to distinguish the one from the other.
Living one day at time,
Enjoying one moment at a time,
Accepting hardship as a pathway to peace.
Taking, as Jesus did, this sinful world as it is
And not as I would have it,
Trusting that You will make all things right
As I surrender to Your will,
That I might be reasonably happy with You in this life
And supremely happy with You forever in the next.
Amen."

PART FIVE:
THE RELATIONAL UPHEAVAL

When a sibling dies, massive change begins to
trickle down into every corner of our lives.

Eventually, if not immediately, we sense the tremors starting to
shake our relationships with family, friends, and coworkers.

People treat us differently.

Some people we counted on disappear.

Others are critical and judgmental.

Still others obviously want to support us but don't know how.

New people show up in our lives.

The relational turnover can be staggering.

In this section, we'll begin to process some of the relational
upheaval that commonly follows the loss of a sister or brother.

For many surviving siblings, this is the most painful
area of their grief journey. Breathe deeply. Take
your time. Use extra pages if you need to.

33

"MY RELATIONSHIPS ARE CHANGING"

"People are being weird. Things are awkward
now. My relationships are changing."

– D.F.

———————————

Sibling loss is an unasked for, unsought, and unwanted force that impacts every area of our lives and brings stressful changes.

The loss of a sister or brother naturally changes us. We're not the same people we were before. Our family is not the same. As a result, this loss also automatically touches all our relationships.

People respond to loss and grief differently. The people around us become aware of what has happened and begin to respond to it in their own ways. We have no control over this.

As a general rule, people don't respond well to loss, emotional pain, and grief. We tend to flee from such things rather than embracing them. Many grieving siblings begin to experience this on some level from their coworkers, friends, and even family members.

Change is a constant in our lives. Sibling loss brings changes we were not expecting and could not fully prepare ourselves for. Almost all of our relationships are jostled in some ways.

Have you sensed some relational shifts since your sibling's death? Describe them.

_____

_____

_____

_____

_____

_____

_____

_____

_____

Do you sense people are looking at you differently now? How so?

_____

_____

_____

_____

_____

_____

_____

_____

Writing Prompts:

Use these prompts to express your heart about some of what's happening in your circle of relationships.

"Since my sibling passed, I've noticed that people..."

_____

_____

_____

_____

_____

_____

_____

"When people see me or hear about my sibling's death, I wish that they would..."

_____

_____

_____

_____

_____

_____

_____

Sibling loss typically brings great relational changes in its wake. Many surviving siblings experience upheaval in even their closest relationships. It's important to process these upsets and expressing what's happening inside you.

34

"I'VE GOTTEN RADICALLY DIFFERENT RESPONSES FROM OTHERS"

"I never know what I'm going to get. I've gotten
radically different responses from others."

– L.L.

The people we encounter will respond differently to us during a time of loss. As you've already discovered, you will meet different kinds of people on your sibling grief journey.

Most people mean well, but what they say and do is unhelpful. They don't know what to say, so they say what they've heard others say. They don't know what to do, so they tend to do nothing.

Some people are fixers. They try to help us feel better. They give advice we haven't asked for. They say and do things that tend to belittle our grief by trying to slap tiny Band-Aids on our gaping wounds. They try to fix the unfixable.

Others are critical judges. They evaluate how they think you're doing and let you know that your behavior is unacceptable. They shake their heads in disgust. They tell us to move on and to get over it.

Some are safe people. They meet us in our grief and accept us as we are. They listen. Their only agenda is to lovingly support us by walking with us as they can.

Still others are fellow grievers. They too are in a season of loss. They can see our pain and relate. They can go beyond sympathy to empathy. Yet, fellow grievers can also be well-meaning but unhelpful. They can be fixers or even judges. They can be safe, supportive people.

You will encounter these five types people on your grief journey. How you respond to them matters.

Think of these five people: the well-meaning but unhelpful person, the fixer, the critical judge, the safe person, and the fellow griever. Have you met all these people since your sibling passed? Try to give an example of each one.

_____

_____

_____

_____

_____

_____

_____

Of these five types of people, which one tends to frustrate you the most? Describe why.

_____

_____

_____

_____

_____

_____

_____

_____

Writing Prompts:

Use the following prompts to dig deeper into your thoughts and feelings about these five types of people.

"As I think of these five types of people I will meet on my grief journey, what comes to mind is..."

_____

_____

_____

_____

_____

_____

_____

"What frustrates me most about how people seem to be responding to me is..."

_____

_____

_____

_____

_____

_____

_____

Memory Writing Exercise:

When you think of the five types of people in this chapter, what memories of your interactions come to mind? Think about your interactions with others since your sibling passed.

_____

_____

_____

_____

_____

_____

_____

_____

Write about the memory above that disturbs you the most. Describe what happened and how you felt. Get it out.

_____

_____

_____

_____

_____

_____

_____

_____

_____

_____

_____

_____

_____

_____

_____

_____

_____

_____

_____

_____

_____

_____

_____

_____

_____

The people around you will respond differently to you during this time. Chances are, this will alter some of your relationships. You are not in control of others' responses. Focus on expressing what's happening inside you as honestly and thoroughly as possible.

35

"WHERE DID EVERYONE GO?"

"People I counted on disappeared.
Poof! Where did everyone go?"

– L.T.

———◦≡◦≡◦———

After a sibling dies, some people disappear on us. One minute they're there expressing sympathy and the next, poof, they're gone.

We count on certain people for support during our grief. We naturally look to our friends, family, and perhaps some others for understanding and comfort. Sadly, some of these people will most likely distance themselves from us in some way. They might say, "We're here for you," but then we never see or hear from them.

These disappearances are common after the death of a sibling. Loss and grief are hard and uncomfortable. Many don't want to even be around emotional pain in any way. Perhaps our grief reminds them of their losses and triggers pain buried in their hearts.

For whatever reason, they don't show up. They were there before, but now they're gone. This relational distancing adds salt to our wounds.

Grief is never about just one loss. One loss brings change that automatically spawns other losses.

Have you experienced people distancing themselves from you since your sibling died? Describe this and how you feel about it:

_____

_____

_____

_____

_____

_____

_____

_____

Why do you think some people have chosen not to show up in your life during this time?

_____

_____

_____

_____

_____

_____

_____

_____

_____

Letter Writing Exercise:

Write a letter to those who have disappeared or distanced themselves from you since your sibling's passing. This is, of course, a letter you will never send. Be honest. Express how you feel. Get it out.

_____

_____

_____

_____

_____

_____

_____

_____

_____

_____

_____

_____

_____

_____

_____

_____

_____

_____

_____

_____

_____

_____

_____

_____

_____

_____

_____

_____

_____

_____

_____

_____

_____

_____

_____

People disappointing us is a common experience on the grief journey. Expressing how you feel about this is important. Don't let the angst and frustration bury itself in your heart. Process these disappearances as best you can, as often as you need to.

36

"WHY CAN'T PEOPLE BE SUPPORTIVE?"

"I expected people to be kind and compassionate. I was mistaken.
Why can't people be supportive?"

– S.W.

———— ◆━◇━◆ ————

It would be nice if everyone we knew was compassionate and supportive. Unfortunately, this is not the case.

Most people will not understand. Perhaps most have not lost siblings. Maybe they've never had a close loss of any kind. Some will not want anything to do with us while we're grieving.

Some will be supportive, but others will not.

We're naturally disappointed and hurt by this. Our broken hearts can be further wounded by people who are close to us and by those we barely know.

At a time when we desperately need care and support, unsupportive people and their responses to us can add to our pain and sense of loss.

Over 3000 years ago, wise King Solomon said, "Above all else, guard your heart, for it is the spring from which everything else in your life flows." Since we can't control how other people react and respond to us and our grief, we must take steps to guard our own hearts.

More on this later.

Have you encountered some unsupportive people in your sibling grief process? List some of the unsupportive comments, body language, and actions that have come at you so far.

_____

_____

_____

_____

_____

_____

_____

When others are unsupportive, how have you responded?

_____

_____

_____

_____

_____

_____

_____

_____

_____

Writing Prompts:

Think of a time where someone was unsupportive, and you walked away hurt and wounded. Use the following prompts to process this event.

"When this happened, I felt..."

_____

_____

_____

_____

_____

_____

_____

"I wish that person could understand that..."

_____

_____

_____

_____

_____

_____

_____

_____

Poetry Writing Exercise:

Using the following list of words, try writing a poem about your interactions with those who have been less than supportive since your sibling died. Let it rip. Express your mind and heart.

Heart   Broken   Pain   Wounded   Shocked

Wish   Angry   Words

_____

_____

_____

_____

_____

_____

_____

_____

_____

_____

_____

_____

_____

_____

_____

_____

_____

_____

_____

_____

_____

_____

_____

_____

_____

_____

_____

_____

Encountering unsupportive people is common for surviving siblings and for grieving hearts in general. Since this is inevitable, we need to find ways to guard our hearts. We can begin to do that by processing these new wounds. We need to "get it out" so that we can begin to release these things and be less affected by them.

37

"AM I EXPECTING TOO MUCH?"

"I expect people to respect my grief. I assume they will be kind.
Am I expecting too much?"

– P.C.

———◆———

Expectations. We all have them.

We have expectations of ourselves, of others, and of the world around us. Others have expectations of us - what we will do and say and how we will behave.

Expectations can be sneaky. We're unaware of many of them. Most expectations go unnoticed and unspoken.

As a result, an expectation is often an invitation to disappointment.

We have expectations of this sibling grief process and how it is going to go.

We have expectations of ourselves and how we will handle all this loss.

We have expectations of how others should respond to us while we're grieving.

When these expectations aren't met and things don't go the way we anticipate, this fuels our angst, frustration, confusion, anxiety, fear, and depression.

We can guard our hearts a little better by identifying and evaluating our expectations of ourselves and others.

After your sibling passed, how did you anticipate your grief process would go? List some of the expectations you had:

_____

_____

_____

_____

_____

_____

_____

_____

Think of a time when a particular expectation you had (of yourself or of others) was not met. Describe what that was like for you:

_____

_____

_____

_____

_____

_____

_____

_____

_____

_____

Writing Prompts:

Use the following prompts to identify and process some of the expectations you have of yourself and others. Write freely whatever comes to mind. Try not to overthink or analyze. Focus on "getting it out."

"Some expectations I have of myself right now are..."

_____

_____

_____

_____

_____

_____

_____

"Some expectations I have of others are..."

_____

_____

_____

_____

_____

_____

_____

Take a few moments and read what you've written. Are these expectations realistic at present? If not, consider how you might release yourself and others from these burdens. Process some of this below:

_____

_____

_____

_____

_____

_____

_____

_____

_____

_____

_____

_____

_____

_____

_____

_____

_____

_____

Memory Writing Exercise:

Since your sibling's death, think of a time when your expectations weren't met. Let the events and interactions around that disappointment surface in your mind.

Write about this memory below. Be as thorough and specific as you can. Express how you felt and what you thought.

_____

_____

_____

_____

_____

_____

_____

_____

_____

_____

_____

_____

_____

_____

_____

_____

_____

_____

_____

_____

_____

_____

_____

_____

_____

_____

_____

_____

_____

_____

_____

_____

_____

_____

Having expectations is natural. The sibling grief journey is already challenging enough without carrying the excess burden of unrealistic expectations. When you find yourself frustrated, angry, or disappointed, ask yourself, "What expectation did I have that was not met?"

Identifying and releasing our expectations is one way we can guard our hearts. This helps us process our grief in healthy ways.

38

"WHERE HAVE ALL THE LISTENERS GONE?"

"I'm tired of being misunderstood, criticized,
and judged. I need support.

Where have all the listeners gone?"

– R.F.

———◆◁◇▷◆———

We all need safe people in our lives, especially when we're grieving the loss of a sister or brother.

Safe people don't evaluate or judge us. They don't give advice we haven't asked for. They don't try to fix the unfixable. They aren't threatened by our grief. They don't make it about themselves.

Safe people meet us where we are and accept us as we are. They are great listeners. They enter our world and exist with us there. They have no agenda other than to support us by being with us in our pain.

Our hearts sense when we're in the presence of a safe person. We begin to relax a little. Just seeing them or hearing their voices can bring relief.

Safe people are key players on this grief journey. They are excellent traveling companions as we traverse this dark, often scary wilderness.

If we don't have any safe people in our lives, we need to find some. They're out there - ready and willing to support us.

Do you have safe people in your life? List their names. Next to each name, describe why they are a safe person to you:

_____

_____

_____

_____

_____

_____

_____

_____

If you don't have safe people in your life, or you need a few more, where do you think you might find them? Brainstorm some options:

_____

_____

_____

_____

_____

_____

_____

_____

_____

_____

Writing Prompts:

Use these prompts to further process this concept of safe people and the role they can play in your life.

"When I think of the safe people in my life, I'm thankful that they..."

_____

_____

_____

_____

_____

_____

Imagine yourself to be a safe person who wants to support other grieving hearts. "As a safe person, I can care for and support others by..."

_____

_____

_____

_____

_____

_____

Safe people aren't perfect. They make mistakes. On the whole, however, they are kind, compassionate, loving, and supportive. They are priceless jewels in this wasteland of grief.

Connect often with your safe people. Your heart needs this.

39

"WORK IS A CHALLENGE"

"Work is a challenge. They expect me to perform
as usual. I'm doing the best I can."

– M.G.

———◦✕◦———

Work relationships can be challenging even when life is fairly steady.
When we're grieving the loss of a sibling, the degree of difficulty at
work tends to go way up.

Fundamentally, work is about performance. We meet the require-
ments of our job and hopefully even exceed them. We strive to meet
the expectations placed upon us. We want to do well.

When a sibling dies, grief begins to gobble up our energy. As grief
takes up more and more space in our lives, there's less of us available
for work. Our performance is naturally affected. Work can provide
some needed distraction from our grief, but the additional weight we
now carry can weigh us down. We're already exhausted and work requires more energy that we don't have.

Our coworkers might be compassionate, for a while. Our bosses,
supervisors, and colleagues will expect us to "return to normal" and
work effectively as soon as possible. Even though our lives have
changed, it's still business as usual for them.

Navigating and managing our work relationships adds an extra
layer of challenge to our already taxed hearts, minds, and bodies.

Have you noticed a change in your work performance since your sibling passed? How so?

_____

_____

_____

_____

_____

_____

_____

_____

How have your boss, supervisor, and coworkers responded to your sibling's death so far?

_____

_____

_____

_____

_____

_____

_____

_____

Writing Prompts:

Use the following prompts to process what's happening at work. Write freely. Jot down whatever comes to mind. Let your heart express itself.

"When I'm at work, I find myself wondering..."

_____

_____

_____

_____

_____

_____

_____

_____

"My coworkers could support me best right now by..."

_____

_____

_____

_____

_____

_____

_____

_____

Letter Writing Exercise:

Write a letter to your boss, supervisor, and work colleagues. What would you like to be able to say to them about your sibling, their death, and what you're experiencing right now? Include how they might support you during this time.

_____

_____

_____

_____

_____

_____

_____

_____

_____

_____

_____

_____

_____

_____

_____

_____

_____

_____

_____

_____

_____

_____

_____

_____

_____

_____

_____

_____

_____

_____

_____

Work relationships can be difficult, especially when we're tired and grieving. If it's possible, consider checking in with your boss or supervisor and share with them how you're doing. You might even want to share the content of the letter you wrote. If they ask how they can support you, tell them.

These conversations can be frightening, but they can also be good and healing. Of course, not every boss or supervisor is even open to such a conversation. Listen to your heart. Be wise. Consult someone safe and trustworthy for their input.

40

"MY SPOUSE IS GETTING FRUSTRATED"

"My spouse is getting frustrated. He is
ready for me to be over this.

How do you get over the death of a brother?"

– M.W.

————◆◇◆————

The loss of a sibling can be hard on marriages and partner relationships.

After a close loss like this, some surviving siblings don't feel supported by their spouses or partners. Instead of compassion and patience, they sense pressure to "get over it" and "move on." They want us "back to normal" and for life to go back to the way it was.

Others grieving siblings feel supported by their life partners but sense a new distance creeping into their relationship. We're changing, and perhaps they don't know what to do with that.

Sibling loss hits our most significant relationships. As we grieve, it will affect our marriage or partner relationship. Our world has been turned upside down. Our family has changed. Our entire relational web is being jostled.

These relational changes can be unnerving and disconcerting. Navigating these changes well is a key part of the sibling grief journey.

Since your sibling's passing, have you noticed changes in your relationship with your spouse or partner? If so, describe these changes:

_____

_____

_____

_____

_____

_____

_____

_____

In your marriage relationship, what are you concerned about at present?

_____

_____

_____

_____

_____

_____

_____

_____

_____

Writing Prompts:

Use these prompts to dig a little deeper into this subject. Be honest. Write freely. Resist the temptation to edit or censor yourself. "Get it out."

"I wonder what my spouse is thinking about..."

_____

_____

_____

_____

_____

_____

_____

"I wish that my partner..."

_____

_____

_____

_____

_____

_____

_____

_____

Letter Writing Exercise:

Write a letter to your spouse or partner about how you would like for them to support you during this time. What do you want them to know about you and your grief? What would be most helpful to you? What do you want and need from them right now?

_____

_____

_____

_____

_____

_____

_____

_____

_____

_____

_____

_____

_____

_____

_____

_____

_____

_____

_____

_____

_____

_____

_____

_____

_____

_____

_____

_____

_____

_____

Consider sharing these things with them. Ask them if they are willing to just listen. Conversations like these can be scary, but they can also be incredibly positive and healing.

A marriage or life partnership takes two to succeed. You have no control over how they respond. All you can do is love them as best you can and share what you can as you walk this rocky road of sibling grief.

41

"I DON'T KNOW HOW TO RELATE TO MY PARENTS NOW"

"I don't know how to relate to my parents now.
Everything is sad, weird, and awkward."

– M.B.

———————◆━◇╳◇━◆———————

The loss of a sibling changes us. As a result, all our relationships are shaken. This includes our relationship with our parents (if they are still living).

Perhaps we are now the only living child. This is a huge change and requires massive adjustment - on the part of both us and our parents.

Maybe we have other surviving siblings. Both siblings and parents are stunned. All of us are hyperaware of who's missing.

We're grieving. Our parents are grieving. Meeting each other in all this upheaval can be hard, awkward, and confusing. Our family has changed forever, and no one knows what to say or how to act.

One thing is certain: our family is different now. Our relationship with our parents will be different. It's almost as if we have to get to know each other all over again.

Have you sensed some changes in your relationship with your parents (or parent)? Try to describe a few of these changes.

_____

_____

_____

_____

_____

_____

_____

_____

_____

_____

_____

_____

_____

_____

_____

_____

_____

_____

Writing Prompts:

Use the prompts below to process the changes you're experiencing in your relationship with your parent(s):

"Since my sibling died, my parent(s) have been..."

_____

_____

_____

_____

_____

_____

_____

"When it comes to my relationship with my parent(s), I wish I could..."

_____

_____

_____

_____

_____

_____

_____

_____

"When I think of my parents, I wonder..."

_____

_____

_____

_____

_____

_____

_____

"I wish my parents would..."

_____

_____

_____

_____

_____

_____

_____

_____

_____

_____

_____

Letter Writing Exercise

Use the space below to write a letter to your parents. What would you like to be able to say to them? What questions do you want to ask them? Express yourself honestly. Don't censor yourself.

_____

_____

_____

_____

_____

_____

_____

_____

_____

_____

_____

_____

_____

_____

_____

_____

_____

_____

_____

_____

_____

_____

_____

_____

_____

_____

_____

_____

_____

_____

_____

_____

_____

_____

Your family is different now. Your relationship with your parents will be different too. You're grieving the loss of your family as you knew it. Processing how things are now is an important part of healing. As you focus on grieving in healthy ways, you will discover how to better relate to your parents as you walk this grief road together.

42

"HOW DO I PARENT AT A TIME LIKE THIS?"

"I know my kids are wondering about me. I'm trying to stay strong for them, but I'm faltering. How do I parent at a time like this?"

– S.B.

Parenting is tough. In fact, it may be one of life's toughest tasks.

In essence, parenting is not so much a task as an ongoing, dynamic relationship. Good parenting, like a good marriage, is a moving target. Things are always changing.

Parenting while grieving the loss of a sibling presents some unique challenges. If our kids are still at home, we're responsible to provide, protect, and lead them amid all the upheaval of this loss. Our desire to "be strong" for them can lead us to stuff our grief and put on a good front. Though this sounds good, it's usually not healthy for us, and it doesn't teach our kids how to handle loss (a skill that they will desperately need).

If our children are adults, they will respond to us and our grief in various ways. Many will try to protect us and fix our grief. Some will get irritated and send signals to us saying, "Get over it and feel better already." Hopefully, some will be compassionate, supportive, and understanding.

In any case, our task is to live from our hearts. That means expressing our grief and what's happening inside us in healthy ways. That includes being honest and open about our grief with our children, according to their age and ability to understand. It's okay and healthy for them to see us express our emotions. By sharing our grief with them, we're modeling some key life skills for them.

Having said this, we also need to be careful about venting and over-sharing with our children, no matter what age they are. They are not our counselors. It isn't their responsibility to rescue us or help us feel better. Like most other things in grief, this calls for wisdom.

Our children will face loss. They already have. We have an opportunity to teach and lead them by how we respond to our loss. This might be uncomfortable or embarrassing for us. That's okay. Grieving in healthy ways in front of our kids is part of loving them well.

How do you sense your children are responding to your grief so far?

_____

_____

_____

_____

_____

What do you wish you could say to your kids about what's happening in your life?

_____

_____

_____

_____

_____

_____

Writing Prompts:

Use the following prompts to write more about parenting during this challenging time.

"When I think about sharing my grief with my children, I wonder about..."

_____

_____

_____

_____

_____

_____

_____

"If I had to guess, I think my kids are looking at me and wondering..."

_____

_____

_____

_____

_____

_____

_____

Memory Writing Exercise:

Think about your interactions with your children since your sibling passed. What conversations and situations come to mind?

_____

_____

_____

_____

_____

_____

_____

Pick one of these memories and write about it below. Describe what happened and what was said. Express what you thought and how you felt:

_____

_____

_____

_____

_____

_____

_____

_____

\
\
\
\
\
\
\
\
\
\
\
\
\
\
\
\
\
\
\
\
\

Your children are experiencing the loss of your sibling as well, no matter what kind of relationship they might have had with them. Consider having a time of sharing memories of your sibling. If your kids are young, you could draw pictures for or about your sibling. Giving your family a chance to grieve together can be a good and precious gift.

43

"FAMILY HAS BEEN A MIXED BAG"

"My family has been a mixed bag since my sister died. Some have been understanding and supportive. Others not so much."

– A.B.

———◦◇◦———

Family can be wonderful. These relationships can also be stressful. When loss and grief get thrown into the mix, some family relationships can be tested.

Some families are incredibly supportive during crisis and loss. Other families are somewhat sympathetic but not helpful. Still others are critical and even toxic.

Most families, however, contain all three of the above. As you grieve the loss of your sibling, it will become apparent who is safe and trustworthy right now and who is not.

As with all relationships, getting around people who are helpful to you and limiting your exposure to those who aren't is key. You can focus on expressing your grief in healthy ways to those who are open to listening and accepting you where we are.

Your family will probably surprise you during this sibling grief journey. Some you thought would be compassionate and supportive may not be. Some you thought would be neutral might step up and become major players during this time.

However family members choose to respond, keep your focus on grieving well. Learning to manage these relationships is an important part of your healing process.

Since your sibling's death, have you noticed any changes in your relationships with other family members? How so?

_____

_____

_____

_____

_____

_____

_____

_____

Looking back, how did you anticipate family members would respond to you and this loss?

_____

_____

_____

_____

_____

_____

_____

_____

_____

Writing Prompts:

Use these prompts to think and write more about your family's role in your sibling grief process.

"When I think about my grief and my family, I am thankful for..."

_____

_____

_____

_____

_____

_____

_____

_____

_____

_____

_____

_____

_____

_____

_____

_____

"When it comes to family members' response to me and my grief, it would be helpful if..."

_____

_____

_____

_____

_____

_____

_____

_____

_____

_____

_____

_____

_____

If you haven't already done so, consider approaching the family members you sense want to be supportive. Tell them a little about what your sibling grief journey is like. Share with them how they can be helpful to you.

Perhaps you're afraid of being disappointed. After all, you're dealing with enough pain as it is. Yet taking a risk like this could be more than worth it. By sharing with trusted family members, you're inviting them into your grief world. That helps them too, more than you may realize.

44

"I THINK I NEED BETTER BOUNDARIES"

"I'm having a tough time with people. Losing
my brother is painful enough.

I think I need better boundaries."

– M.D.

———⋅⊂◇⊃⋅———

This world is not kind to hearts - especially grieving hearts.

When a sibling dies, we're stunned and even paralyzed for a time.
Life keeps blazing forward with stunning speed. We get dragged along
with it, kicking and screaming.

No one likes grief and pain. We avoid such things at all costs.

Grieving in healthy ways demands that we guard our hearts. We do
that by expressing honestly what's happening inside us. We connect
with people who are helpful to us and limit our exposure to those who
aren't. We pursue practices and habits that lead to healing and overall
wellness.

Making sure our hearts get the nurturing they need is a massive
part of our recovery and healing. At a time when our tank is nearly
always empty, we need good, healthy inflow. We welcome messages
and influences that are truthful, loving, and compassionate. We begin
to weed out information and influences that are upsetting, confusing,
and toxic to our grief process.

We need to guard our "eye gate" and our "ear gate." We can't
un-see or unhear something. We're profoundly impacted by what we

take in. This is a time when we need to be vigilant about what we choose to expose ourselves to.

What do you need in your life right now? Comfort? Acceptance? Love? Peace? Hope? Meaning? Faith? Reassurance?

_____

_____

_____

_____

_____

_____

_____

_____

Seek what you need. What kind of information, people, and influences are healthy for you and can meet your needs? Write down who and what comes to mind:

_____

_____

_____

_____

_____

_____

_____

_____

"Guard your heart." What do you think of when you read this phrase?

_____

_____

_____

_____

_____

_____

_____

_____

What are some influences (and people) that you know are not healthy for you right now?

_____

_____

_____

_____

_____

_____

_____

_____

_____

Writing Prompts:

Use these prompts to delve more into what it might mean to guard your heart during this season of sibling grief.

"When I think of things or people who might nurture me and help heal my wounded heart, I think of..."

_____

_____

_____

_____

_____

_____

_____

"When it comes to guarding my eye gate and ear gate, I think I need to..."

_____

_____

_____

_____

_____

_____

_____

_____

Poetry Writing Exercise:

Using the following list of words, try writing a poem about guarding your heart. Feel free to use any other words you wish in addition to these. Don't overthink it. Don't worry about rhyme, meter, or composition.

Heart   Soul   Guard   Protect   Nurture

Heal   Wound   Pain   Grief   Afraid

Courage   Grow   Time

_____

_____

_____

_____

_____

_____

_____

_____

_____

_____

_____

_____

_____

_____

_____

_____

_____

_____

_____

_____

_____

_____

_____

_____

_____

_____

_____

_____

_____

_____

_____

_____

_____

Your heart is the core of who you are. Guard it well. Nurture it. You're more important than you realize.

PART SIX:
THE FOGGY FUTURE

When we lose a sibling, the future we anticipated changed.

We don't realize this at first. With each passing day, however, we become increasingly aware of the domino effect this loss has had on our hopes, dreams, and expectations.

Our future might now appear dark and foggy.
We wonder what's out there for us.

What will we do?

What will life be like?

Who will we be now?

In this section, we'll begin to dig into how your sibling's death has impacted your future.

As you move through these pages, practice breathing deeply from time to time. You may discover things you had not thought of or realized before.

Be honest. Use extra pages as necessary. Focus on expressing your grief and "getting it out."

45

"THE FUTURE IS DIFFERENT NOW"

"Nothing is the same. The future is different now."

– R.E.

When we lose a sibling, what we don't realize at the time is that our future has just been significantly altered. Depending on our family situation, the future we anticipated may be gone.

We all have expectations. Most of these are subconscious, automatic, and unspoken. Though we might not have ever talked about them, chances are we have many assumptions about the future. We count on certain things and people, without even realizing it.

When a sibling dies, we suddenly discover that the landscape ahead of us has changed. The world looks the same, but things are different now. A key piece of our life puzzle is missing.

Part of the sibling grief journey includes coming face-to-face with a future that is now different from what you anticipated. This can bring a profound sense of more loss.

You not only mourn the loss of your sister or brother, but also of everything attached to them, including your future expectations.

Before your sibling's passing, what assumptions did you have about the future? Make a list of the things you anticipated that included your sibling.

_____

_____

_____

_____

_____

_____

_____

Out of your list above, choose three of the most painful losses. Write these lost expectations down again here. Beside each one, express a little about how you feel about that loss.

_____

_____

_____

_____

_____

_____

_____

_____

Writing Prompts:

Use the following prompts to process more about the future you anticipated. Try not to edit as you write. Express your thoughts freely.

"When I look at the future now, I wonder..."

_____

_____

_____

_____

_____

_____

_____

"Some of the expectations I have now about the future are..."

_____

_____

_____

_____

_____

_____

The reality is that each day is new. Every moment is uncharted territory. You have never been in this particular place at this time. Change is one thing you can always count on. Part of grieving well includes learning to hold all things loosely and to live in the present as much as possible. Expressing your grief about the loss of what you expected is important.

46

"SOME OF WHAT I HOPED FOR IS NO LONGER POSSIBLE"

"I look down the road now and things are foggy. With my brother gone, some of what I hoped for is no longer possible."

– L.R.

———————

As we said in the last chapter, when we lose a sibling, we also lose much of what was attached to them. Most likely, this includes some of our hopes and dreams.

At best, our future hopes that included our sibling are now significantly altered. At worst, these hopes are shattered, crushed, and gone.

Our future hopes and dreams might have included certain relationships, places, houses, and financial circumstances. Perhaps certain scenarios about what we would do, where we would go, and what we would experience were in the mix.

Our sibling will not come home again. They will no longer go to work. They will not come around the corner. They will not attend future births, graduations, weddings, or other special events. They will not be there when we need them. Every mental image we have of the future that included our sibling has now been altered or has disappeared.

When we lose a sister or brother, we not only grieve what we lost, but also what will now never be in this life. This can be painful and disorienting. Being kind to ourselves in this process is crucial.

What are some of things you hoped for in the future that have now changed? Make a list of them here:

_____

_____

_____

_____

_____

_____

_____

From the list above, which lost hope or dream is the most painful for you right now? Describe this loss and the pain you feel about it:

_____

_____

_____

_____

_____

_____

_____

_____

_____

_____

_____

_____

_____

_____

_____

_____

_____

_____

_____

_____

_____

_____

_____

_____

_____

_____

_____

_____

_____

_____

Letter Writing Exercise:

Write a letter to your sibling. Tell them what you're going to miss about the future. Share the hopes and dreams that you had. Express your heart, as honestly as you can.

_____

_____

_____

_____

_____

_____

_____

_____

_____

_____

_____

_____

_____

_____

_____

_____

_____

_____

_____

_____

_____

_____

_____

_____

_____

_____

_____

_____

_____

_____

_____

Acknowledging and identifying lost hopes and dreams is an important part of the grief journey. Expressing your thoughts and feelings about these future losses is part of taking care of yourself and honoring your sibling.

Breathe deeply. This journey is a one step, one moment at a time process.

47

"AM I ALWAYS GOING TO GRIEVE?"

"Out of the blue I get hit by a grief wave – again.
How long is this going to go on?

Am I always going to grieve?"

– A.M.

———————⚬◇⚬———————

There are times in the sibling grief process where we sense we're healing. We believe we're doing better.

Then we experience another grief attack. Emotions overwhelm us, and we feel like we're right back where we started. It can seem like we're losing our sibling all over again.

Sudden grief bursts months and even years after a loss are natural and common.

We're minding our own business and suddenly a grief lightning bolt strikes. Many times, we can identify a trigger of some sort - a person, voice, place, aroma, song, holiday, family event, death anniversary, etc. Other times, it feels like we got hit by the grief bus from behind without warning.

Grief bursts can be good and healing. The grief is within us and needs to be expressed. These sudden floods of emotion provide a pressure release for our hearts. The spillways of our grief reservoir open and what's inside comes cascading out.

One thing that can help is to proactively prepare for these surges in grief. We can develop some exit strategies.

Option A might be to simply leave where we are and go to a

private place (a restroom, our car, etc.). Then we breathe deeply and decide what we want to do.

Option B might be to stay where we are, breathe deeply, and see if we can continue being where we are and doing what we're doing.

Being proactive and giving ourselves a couple of options can be vastly relieving and helpful when grief bursts come.

Some find it helpful to carry a note with a few calming words in their wallet. Others might memorize a peace-giving scripture or quote.

We let the grief come. We feel it through. We process it as best we can. We're not going backwards. Grief bursts are unpredictable in the sense that they can happen anytime, anywhere, but they are natural and common.

Describe what a grief burst is like for you. Describe your feelings and thoughts during that time:

_____

_____

_____

_____

_____

_____

_____

_____

_____

_____

_____

_____

What do you think about Option A and B above as proactive possibilities for when grief bursts strike? Can you think of any more options? Try picturing yourself in a public place and having a grief burst. See yourself applying your options.

_____

_____

_____

Writing Prompts:

Use the following prompts to write more about grief bursts and how you would like to handle them.

"When I have a grief burst, I get concerned about..."

_____

_____

_____

_____

_____

_____

"When a grief burst comes, I would like to be able to..."

_____

_____

_____

_____

_____

_____

Grief bursts are common and natural. They can be triggered by anything at any time. When they come, find time to process them, if you can.

Please don't view grief bursts as steps back. Your heart is expressing itself. Give your heart space to do so. Accept yourself as best you can in the moment.

48

"HOLIDAYS ARE GOING TO BE DIFFERENT"

"Her birthday was last week. That rattled me.
Holidays are sure going to be different."

– P.W.

———————◆◇◆———————

Special days fill our calendars. Birthdays. Anniversaries. Christmas. Thanksgiving. Holidays. Though these days are normally joyful, for grieving siblings these times can extremely difficult.

Holidays and special days can surface the loss of our sibling like nothing else. As these days approach, we become hyperaware of who's missing. When the special day comes, we bump into a memory with every step.

Navigating these times can be exhausting and challenging. The dread of these days alone can suck us dry and immobilize us.

As with the rest of the sibling grief process, we need to find ways to process these times. The good news is that instead of hiding and hoping for the best (which never works well), we can resolve to meet these days with courage and use them to honor our sibling and to express our grief in meaningful ways.

The most important thing is to be proactive and make a simple plan for the day to remember our sibling and to honor them.

Since your sibling died, what special days have been difficult for you? Describe what those days were like.

_____

_____

_____

_____

_____

_____

_____

_____

As you look ahead, what special days are lurking in front of you? Which ones are you most concerned about and why?

_____

_____

_____

_____

_____

_____

_____

_____

Writing Prompts:

Use these prompts to process more about upcoming special days and how you can meet them well.

"When I think of the special days ahead, some things I might do to remember and honor my sibling are..." (Brainstorm a list of possibilities):

_____

_____

_____

_____

_____

_____

"With regard to the next special day coming up, I'm concerned that..."

_____

_____

_____

_____

_____

_____

_____

_____

Don't ignore upcoming holidays and special days. Guard your heart by being proactive and making a simple plan to take care of yourself and honor your sibling that day.

IDEAS FOR HOLIDAYS AND SPECIAL OCCASIONS

Instead of dreading special days – anniversaries, birthdays, and holidays – focus on being proactive about these times and using them for good.

Here are a few ideas to help you take care of yourself and honor your sibling on these difficult days:

- Light a candle in their honor.

- Make a donation in their name.

- Serve in a cause that they were passionate about.

- Write them a letter telling them how much you love them and what you're thankful for.

- Invite a few others who knew your loved one to participate in a time of memory sharing.

- Remember and honor them by giving gifts to others in their name on their birthday or death anniversary.

- Set up a scholarship fund in their name.

- Set up an empty chair in remembrance of them at family gatherings and other special occasions.

- Intentionally include them in gatherings on holidays by inviting everyone to share something about them.

- Have a birthday party for them and ask others to bring a card that reminds them of your loved one. Have those attending share a memory or story.

- Host a butterfly release on the anniversary of their death.

- Give some of their possessions to others as items of remembrance.

Get creative. Think about your loved one. What do you think might bring a smile to their face?

_____

_____

_____

_____

_____

_____

_____

_____

_____

_____

_____

_____

_____

Pay attention to your heart. Use these special days to help you adjust, recover, heal, and grow.

49

"WHO AM I NOW?"

"I never realized just how important my sister was
in my life. I feel lost. Who am I now?"

– B.E.

———————— ❖ ————————

After the loss of a sibling, our sense of identity can be shaken. Some losses change so much that we can wonder who we are now and what we're supposed to do.

We have many roles in life: child, sibling, student, parent, relative, friend, caregiver, employee, boss, citizen, organization member, etc. When a sibling dies, many of these roles are greatly affected and one is perhaps completely erased. Though we are not what we do, we naturally connect some of our more important roles with who we are.

Our sense of who we are is key to how we live life. We live out and daily express who we truly believe ourselves to be. Our sense of identity is a major driver of our thoughts, emotions, and purpose. Having something taken from us that shakes our basic sense of who we are can be frightening.

Having at least some bit of identity crisis during a season of loss is common for grieving siblings. Processing the impact of our sibling's death on who we perceive ourselves to be is important.

List some of the roles you have in life (child, sibling, student, parent, relative, friend, caregiver, employee, boss, citizen, organization member, etc.):

_____

_____

_____

_____

_____

_____

_____

Which of these roles has been affected by your sibling's passing? Describe some of the changes.

_____

_____

_____

_____

_____

_____

_____

_____

_____

Writing Prompts:

Use the following prompts to write about how your sibling's death has affected your sense of who you are.

"I'm not the same person I was before. For example, now..."

_____

_____

_____

_____

_____

_____

"If I had to answer the question, 'Who am I?', I would say..."

_____

_____

_____

_____

_____

_____

Sibling loss shakes our lives. It alters our families and our personal worlds. Our sense of who we are can be jostled and upended.

All of this is incredibly stressful. Breathe deeply. Be kind to yourself. Focus on "getting the grief out" in healthy ways. Live life one step, one moment at a time.

50

"I USED TO BE A DECENT DECISION-MAKER"

"I used to be a decent decision-maker. Since the death of my sister, I find myself hesitating. It's like I'm scared of making a mistake."

– T.P.

———————————

Making decisions is normally stressful and challenging. While we're grieving the loss of a sibling, decision-making can seem frightening and even impossible.

After a sibling's passing, our lives are anything but business as usual. There is more flux and change going on than we realize. Our world is shifting. We tend to be out of balance in many ways.

Simple wisdom tells us to let things settle before making any big, life-altering decisions. Most recommend that we avoid making any major decisions for six months to a year.

When time-sensitive, large decisions must be made, we need to make certain we don't make them alone. We need to involve other people we trust who have expertise and wisdom in those areas.

Many grieving siblings experience decision-making paralysis. Even the smallest decision - like what to have for dinner - can be overwhelming. The loss of a sibling can catapult us into being hyper-careful about everything. We don't want to make any mistakes. We can't handle any extra trouble right now.

At times, we might be tempted to make quick, impulsive decisions. Making decisions is one way we can take action and "do something" to try and quell the underlying terror of feeling out of control. These quick, impulsive actions rarely produce good results, especially if they are big, life-changing decisions.

In our world, we are used to everything being fast and convenient. The sibling grief process is neither. Grief cannot be hurried or pushed.

Recovery and healing are not goals that can be achieved by a checklist of actions and activities. The grief journey is not a straight sprint down a minor stretch of the highway of life. It is more like a meandering marathon through a thick, overgrown forest.

Since your sibling's death, what has decision-making been like for you? Describe this:

_____

_____

_____

_____

_____

_____

_____

_____

_____

_____

_____

_____

_____

What decisions do you sense are looming in front of you? Make a list of them here (even "small" decisions can be stressful!).

_____

_____

_____

_____

_____

_____

_____

_____

_____

_____

_____

_____

_____

_____

_____

_____

_____

Letter Writing Exercise:

Write a letter to yourself about decision-making. Detach and pretend that you are a trusted friend and wise mentor. What would you say to yourself about decision-making in the months ahead? Write freely. Resist the temptation to edit. Be honest.

_____

_____

_____

_____

_____

_____

_____

_____

_____

_____

_____

_____

_____

_____

_____

_____

_____

_____

_____

_____

_____

_____

_____

_____

_____

_____

_____

_____

_____

_____

Take your time. Let patience rule. Resist making the big decisions that don't absolutely have to be made right then. Don't be rushed or bullied by others in this process. Guard your heart.

51

"WHY AM I HERE?"

"Maybe I didn't think very deeply before. Now, I find myself
wondering about the meaning of life. Why am I here?"

– N.W.

———————•◇•———————

A sibling's death can upend our lives to the point that even our purpose
can be called into question. We can wonder who we are and why we're
here. We can find ourselves thinking, "What's the point anyway?"

Wondering about our purpose and mission is natural and common
for those on the sibling grief journey. If we're willing, this loss can
help us further clarify who we are and what life is all about. This grief
journey can fine tune our personal missions and move us to live with
more passion and purpose than ever before.

When we lack a strong sense of purpose, our hearts go into hiding.
We become like a piece of wood thrown into a river with a swift current. We get swept along, bobbing here and there, getting slammed
against the rocks along the way. We're alive and making good time,
but we don't know where we're going.

The sibling grief journey gives us a unique opportunity to reevalu-
ate our lives, including our purpose and direction. Our hearts have
been broken. Life is different now. This is a time of questioning and
change. Rather than simply being swept along, we can pay attention to
what our hearts are saying to us.

Whatever our purpose might be, it will be closely connected to
three things: people, love, and service. We're designed for relationship. We're wired to love and be loved. We're all interdependent on
each other. We're in this together.

Since your sibling's passing, have you wondered about your purpose and mission in life (who you are and why you're here)? How so?

_____

_____

_____

_____

_____

_____

_____

_____

At this point, what would you say is your purpose in life? Why are you here?

_____

_____

_____

_____

_____

_____

_____

_____

_____

Writing Prompts:

Use the following prompts to process more about your mission in life and why you're here. Remember to write freely and try not to edit or censor yourself as you go.

"If I had to put it into words, I would say that the meaning of life is..."

_____

_____

_____

_____

_____

_____

_____

_____

"I can use this loss to help me live out my purpose and mission by..."

_____

_____

_____

_____

_____

_____

_____

_____

Letter Writing Exercise:

Write a letter from your sibling to yourself about your mission in life. What would they say to you about your purpose in life and why you are here?

_____

_____

_____

_____

_____

_____

_____

_____

_____

_____

_____

_____

_____

_____

_____

_____

Without a clear sense of purpose, we wander. We end up chasing things that don't matter. We pile up regrets. We allow the world around us to set the agenda rather than our internal priorities and values. Sibling loss can teach us to dig deeper and to pay more attention to our hearts.

Part of processing our grief in healthy ways is reevaluating who we really are and becoming even more clear about our mission and purpose.

52

"I WANT TO MAKE THIS COUNT"

"I want to find ways to use all this for
good. I want to make this count."

– D.A.

―――――――◦✕◦――――――

For many grieving siblings, the thing that helps most in their grief process is finding ways to use their pain for good.

Sibling grief can be overwhelming. We need breaks. We need to get out of our own heads for a while. Noticing those around us and serving others can temporarily focus our attention elsewhere. We get the small grief breaks we need and accomplish something meaningful. Others benefit, and we can see some of the fruit of our actions.

Serving others brings perspective. When we give, we end up receiving. When we serve, we heal a little.

Connecting with others and serving gives purpose to our pain. We're reminded that we're in this together.

Service exercises our broken hearts. We need this kind of exercise to be healthy. In times of pain and loss, we need to find ways to live with purpose.

Again, what our personal mission is, it will boil down to people, love, and service.

How can we begin to use our grief for good?

Are there ways we can serve those around us - our family, neighbors, friends, and coworkers?

Is there a cause or organization we might volunteer with?

Can we support other grieving hearts somehow?

Though our tank is low to empty, we need to reach out in service. Rather than draining us further, this actually puts a little back into our tank.

How might you serve others during this time? Brainstorm a list of possibilities. Get creative. Think outside the box.

_____

_____

_____

_____

_____

_____

_____

_____

Of the things you listed above, which ones are the most attractive to you?

_____

_____

_____

_____

_____

_____

_____

_____

Writing Prompts:

Use the following prompts to talk more about serving others during your time of grief.

"When I think about serving others right now, I feel..."

_____

_____

_____

_____

_____

_____

_____

_____

"When it comes to reaching out and serving others, I am willing to..."

_____

_____

_____

_____

_____

_____

_____

_____

_____

_____

_____

_____

_____

_____

_____

_____

_____

_____

_____

_____

_____

_____

_____

Using our grief for good is a key part of the healing process. Serving others helps us process our own grief better. Loving those around us - perhaps just by noticing them and expressing care for them - can bring perspective and comfort.

When we serve while grieving, everyone wins.

CONCLUDING THOUGHTS

The loss of a sister or brother is painful. The sibling grief journey is challenging and exhausting. Processing the grief inside and "getting it out" is key to recovery, adjustment, healing, and growth.

In this workbook, you've moved through various aspects of the grief process. You've engaged your heart in expressing what's happening inside you. You've tackled difficult issues, circumstances, and relationships.

The grief work you've done matters. Your heart, mind, body, and soul have all benefited. Your relationships will be enriched as well, if that isn't happening already!

Every step toward healing is a step forward.

Be kind to yourself.

Be patient with yourself.

Keep writing.

Make writing a daily habit.

Keep expressing what's happening inside you. Keep giving your heart avenues to vent and share.

As you travel this grief road, accept yourself as you are in the moment.

Accept others as they are. Get around people who are helpful to you and limit your exposure to those who aren't.

Guard and nurture your heart.

As you grieve well, seek to love well. Let your compassion deepen.

Use your grief for good. Make serving others a habit.

Keep this workbook / journal handy. Refer to it as needed. Engage in the writing exercises again. You'll be encouraged by how you've healed and grown.

I'm honored to be with you on this journey. Please visit me at www.garyroe.com. Feel free to contact me and share. I'm here to help, if I can.

And remember: You're not alone, you're not crazy, and you will make it through this.

Warmly,
Gary

Don't forget to download your free eBook (PDF):

Grief: 9 Things I Wish I Had Known

https://www.garyroe.com/grief-9-thingsi-wish-i-had-known-ebook

ADDITIONAL GRIEF RESOURCES

THE COMFORT SERIES

www.garyroe.com/comfort-series

Comfort for Grieving Hearts: Hope and Encouragement in Times of Loss

Comfort for the Grieving Spouse's Heart: Hope and Healing After Losing Your Partner

Comfort for the Grieving Adult Child's Heart: Hope and Healing After Losing Your Parent

Comfort for the Grieving Parent's Heart: Hope and Healing After Losing Your Child

THE GOD AND GRIEF SERIES

www.garyroe.com/god-and-grief-series

Grief Walk: Experiencing God After the Loss of a Loved One

Widowed Walk: Experiencing God After the Loss of a Spouse

Broken Walk: Experiencing God After the Loss of a Child

Orphaned Walk: Experiencing God After the Loss of a Parent (coming soon)

THE GOOD GRIEF SERIES

https://www.garyroe.com/good-grief-series/

The Grief Guidebook: Common Questions,
Compassionate Answers, Practical Suggestions

www.garyroe.com/grief-guidebook

Aftermath: Picking Up the Pieces After a Suicide

www.garyroe.com/aftermath

Shattered: Surviving the Loss of a Child

www.garyroe.com/shattered

Teen Grief: Caring for the Grieving Teenage Heart

www.garyroe.com/teengrief

Please Be Patient, I'm Grieving: How to Care
for and Support the Grieving Heart

www.garyroe.com/please-be-patient

Heartbroken: Healing from the Loss of a Spouse

www.garyroe.com/heartbroken-2

Surviving the Holidays Without You: Navigating
Loss During Special Seasons

www.garyroe.com/surviving-the-holidays

THE DIFFERENCE MAKER SERIES

www.garyroe.com/difference-maker

Difference Maker: Overcoming Adversity and Turning
Pain into Purpose, Every Day (Adult & Teen Editions)

Living on the Edge: How to Fight and Win the Battle
for Your Mind and Heart (Adult & Teen Editions)

FREE ON GARY'S WEBSITE

Grief: 9 Things I Wish I had Known

In this deeply personal and practical eBook, Gary shares nine key lessons from his own grief journeys. "This was so helpful! I saw myself on every page," said one reader. "I wish I had read this years ago," said another. Widely popular, this eBook has brought hope and comfort to thousands of grieving hearts.

Available at www.garyroe.com

The Good Grief Mini-Course

Full of personal stories, inspirational content, and practical assignments, this 8-session email series is designed to help readers understand grief and deal with its roller-coaster emotions. Thousands have been through this course, which is now being used in support groups as well.

Available at www.garyroe.com.

The Hole in My Heart: Tackling Grief's Tough Questions

This eBook tackles some of grief's big questions: "How did this happen?" "Why?" "Am I crazy?" "Am I normal?" "Will this get any easier?" plus others. Written in the first person, it engages and comforts the heart.

Available at www.garyroe.com.

I Miss You: A Holiday Survival Kit

Thousands have downloaded this brief, easy-to-read, and very personal e-book. I Miss You provides some basic, simple tools on how to use holiday and special times to grieve well and love those around you.

Available at www.garyroe.com.

A REQUEST FROM THE AUTHOR

Thank you for taking your heart seriously and working through *Grieving the Write Way for Siblings*. I hope you found some comfort, healing, and practical help in these pages.

I would love to hear what you thought of this book. Would you consider taking a moment and sending me a few sentences on how *Grieving the Write Way for Siblings* impacted you?

Send me your thoughts at contact@garyroe.com.

Your comments and feedback mean a lot to me and will assist me in producing more quality resources for grieving hearts.

Thank you.

Warmly,

Gary

Help us reach other grieving hearts.

Share this link:

https://www.garyroe.com/grieving-the-write-way-series

ABOUT THE AUTHOR

Gary's story began with a childhood of mixed messages and sexual abuse. This was followed by other losses and numerous grief experiences.

Ultimately, a painful past led Gary into a life of helping wounded people heal and grow. A former college minister, missionary in Japan, entrepreneur in Hawaii, pastor, and hospice chaplain, he now serves as a writer, speaker, grief specialist, and grief coach.

In addition to *Grieving the Write Way for Siblings*, Gary is the author of more than 20 books, including the award-winning bestsellers *The Grief Guidebook, Shattered: Surviving the Loss of a Child, Comfort for the Grieving Spouse's Heart,* and *Aftermath: Picking Up the Pieces After a Suicide*. Gary's books have won four international book awards and have been named finalists seven times. He has been featured on Dr. Laura, Belief Net, the Christian Broadcasting Network, Wellness, Thrive Global, and other major media and has well over 800 grief-related articles in print. Recipient of the Diane Duncam Award for Excellence in Hospice Care, Gary is a popular keynote, conference, and seminar speaker at a wide variety of venues.

Gary loves being a husband and father. He has seven adopted children. He enjoys hockey, corny jokes, good puns, and colorful Hawaiian shirts. Gary and his wife Jen and family live in Texas.

Visit Gary at www.garyroe.com.

Don't forget to download your free eBook (PDF):

Grief: 9 Things I Wish I Had Known

https://www.garyroe.com/
grief-9-things-i-wish-i-had-known-ebook/

ACKNOWLEDGMENTS

Special thanks for my amazing wife Jen for her constant support and encouragement. Thank you for partnering with me in helping grieving hearts heal and grow.

Thanks to my wonderful Advance Reader Team for their corrections, feedback, and input. You make every book much better.

Thanks to Glendon Haddix of Streetlight Graphics for his artistic skill and expertise in design and formatting. Your artistry continues to bring healing and hope to many.

AN URGENT PLEA
HELP OTHER GRIEVING HEARTS

Dear Reader,

Others are hurting and grieving today. You can help.

How?

With a simple, heartfelt review.

Could you take a few moments and write a 1-3 sentence review of *Grieving the Write Way for Siblings* and leave it on the site you purchased the book from?

And if you want to help even more, you could leave the same review on the *Grieving the Write Way for Siblings* book page on Goodreads.

Your review counts and will help reach others who could benefit from this book.

Thanks for considering this. I read these reviews as well, and your comments and feedback assist me in producing more quality resources for grieving hearts.

Thank you!

Warmly,

Gary

Don't forget to download your free eBook (PDF):

Grief: 9 Things I Wish I Had Known

https://www.garyroe.com/
grief-9-things-i-wish-i-had-known-ebook

Made in the USA
Monee, IL
06 January 2024

51310378R00163